THE LAST TIME
I WORE A DRESS

THE LAST TIME I WORE A DRESS

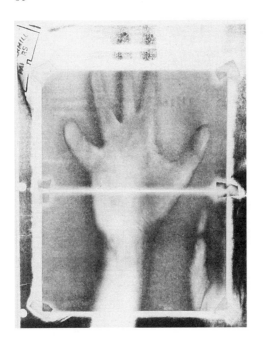

DAPHNE SCHOLINSKI
WITH JANE MEREDITH ADAMS

RIVERHEAD BOOKS
A MEMBER OF PENGUIN PUTNAM INC.
NEW YORK
1997

RIVERHEAD BOOKS
a member of
Penguin Putnam Inc.
200 Madison Avenue
New York, NY 10016

The diagnostic criteria for Gender Identity Disorder appearing on
p. 205 is reprinted with permission from the *Diagnostic and Statistical
Manual of Mental Disorders*, Fourth Edition. Copyright © 1994
American Psychiatric Association.

Library of Congress Cataloging-in-Publication Data

Scholinski, Daphne.
    The last time I wore a dress / by Daphne Scholinski, with Jane
Meredith Adams.
        p.   cm.
    ISBN 1-57322-077-9
    1. Scholinski, Daphne—Health.   2. Gender identity disorders—
Patients—United States—Biography.   I. Adams, Jane Meredith.
II. Title.
RC560.G45S34   1997
616.85'83—dc21   97-17321 CIP
[B]

Printed in the United States of America

10   9   8   7   6   5   4   3   2   1

This book is printed on acid-free paper.   ∞

Book design by Marysarah Quinn

I've told my story as honestly as I can. Some people might tell a different story about what happened to me, but this is what I know to be true. In order to protect the privacy of the people involved, most of their names have been changed.

FOR EVERYONE

PROLOGUE

EVEN NOW, it's always the same question: Why don't you act more like a girl? Makeup, dresses, a little swing in my walk is what people mean. The millennium is upon us and this is the level of discussion.

The only thing I can say is, I tried.

It wasn't as simple as my doctors made it sound. In the hospital, I turned control of my face over to my roommate Donna, a fluffy-haired girl with major depression. She wanted to help. She tried to pinpoint exactly why my fifteen-year-old girl-face looked boyish. This turned out to be a bigger question than we could answer.

So we settled for the superficial: A jawline that needed shading? Eyes that needed definition?

Donna wasn't given the strong drugs, at least not early in the morning, so her aim was true. She came at me with a black wand and drew a thin line on the edge of my eyelid.

From the bed my other roommate piped up. "You have wicked lashes." Mostly she kept quiet, since she was not too naturally feminine-appearing herself, and wanted to stay out of the mess I was in.

Every morning I lowered my eyelids and let Donna make me up. If I didn't emerge from my room with foundation, lip gloss, blush, mascara, eyeliner, eye shadow and feathered hair, I lost points. Without points, I couldn't go to the dining room, I couldn't go anywhere, not that we were going many places to begin with. Without points, I was not allowed to walk from the classroom back to the unit without an escort. The teacher handed me off to an attendant who asked what did you learn in school today and isn't English literature wonderful and I could tell by his voice he thought it was a pathetic thing to be a girl who didn't have enough points to travel a hundred feet alone. Either choice I hated: makeup, or a man trailing in my shadow. It didn't take me long to figure out that a half-moon of blue on my eyelids was a better decision. This was how I learned what it means to be a woman.

When Donna stepped back, I stared in the mirror at the girl who was me, and not me: the girl I was supposed to be.

"I like my blue eye shadow," I said. Through the slightly open door I knew George, the counselor with a wrestler's build, listened in the hall. During the day, we almost always had to have our doors open. To inspire me they sent over the gorgeous male counselors.

"I really like my eyeliner," I said. Ever lied to save yourself? "I love looking pretty." Ever been so false your own skin is your enemy?

No affirmations, no points. I knew that later my counselor would put a check mark next to my morning treatment goal: "Spend 15 minutes with a female peer combing and curling hair and experimenting with makeup." Ten points, as long as I showered and washed my hair first.

The staff was under orders to scrutinize my femininity: the way I walked, the way I sat with my ankle on my knee, the clothes I wore, the way I kept my hair. Trivial matters, one might say. But trivial matters in which the soul reveals itself. Try changing these things. Try it.

Wear an outfit that is utterly foreign—a narrow skirt when what you prefer is a loose shift of a dress. Torn-up black jeans when what you like are pin-striped wool trousers. See how far you can contradict your nature. Feel how your soul rebels.

One million dollars my treatment cost. Insurance money, but still. Three years in three mental hospitals for girly lessons, 1981–1984. A high-school diploma from a psychiatric facility for adolescents, a document I never show anyone.

Donna had a knack for eyeliner and strawberry-flavored lip gloss but for the price, I would have thought they'd bring in someone really good, maybe Vidal Sassoon.

ONE

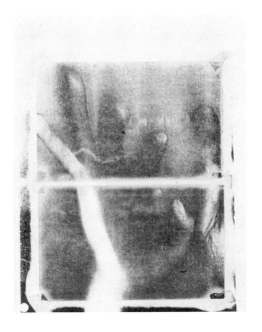

SEPTEMBER 10, 1981:

My father and I left Arlington Heights,

Illinois, with my gray, hard-sided

Samsonite in the backseat. Heading east on

a flat stretch of I-90, destined for Chicago,

we rode in uncompanionable silence, which

was a shame, since underneath our

loathing, we'd liked each other once.

My father drove a brown Cutlass, neatly kept, the car of a family man, which was a role he aspired to but had trouble filling. He blamed his paternal failings on me. The set of my chin was irresistible to his palm. Like him, I couldn't stop myself once we'd begun. One night he discovered that I'd taped pinups of Shaun Cassidy and Erik Estrada floor-to-ceiling on my bedroom wall. *That tape is going to peel the paint off*, he announced, pacing through my room while my mind floated near sleep. I hoped he'd go away and leave Shaun Cassidy alone. He kept at it about the tape and the peeling paint until I sat up in bed and yelled, *Get out of my room*, and he yelled, *No*. I pulled the pictures off into a heap. I tried not to rip them but even in the darkness I could see Erik Estrada had a tear through his forehead that made him look like Frankenstein.

It got worse. Years later he'd say, *You took the backgammon board to your friend's, you know you're not allowed to take that out of the house*, and I'd walk up to him close enough so that his angry face was all I could see of the world, and he'd push me away, so I'd push back, and we were off. He shouted with his jugular vein sticking out, his throat red from the blood rushing through, and I shouted, *How was I supposed to know I couldn't take the backgammon set?* until he rushed at me with his forefinger extended like a nail. He poked me on the chest, thud, thud, until I cried. *Go ahead, hit me. I know you want to*, I taunted. This was thrilling. If he hit me, I'd won—I'd cracked him open and reached his center.

His palm flew out and caught my cheek.

My behavior mystified him. He wanted a demure and obedient daughter, like my younger sister, Jean. She saw the twisty path I was on and ran in the other direction. She vowed never to talk back to an adult and to send her allowance money to a puffy-haired preacher on tv. Which was why she was a free eleven-year-old who tucked her Snoopy and her Magic Eight Ball into bed at night and I was here with him, arms folded across my chest, driving to meet my fate.

My father wasn't always touchy and violent. "Night and day," my mother would say—that's how my father was, before and after Vietnam. It took me a while to figure out that Vietnam meant a war and that people died. When I asked my father if he'd killed anyone, his face changed, a window shut, and he spoke in a robot voice. "Well, yeah," he said, looking at a point somewhere over my shoulder.

My mother was seventeen and pregnant with me when he came back with shrapnel studding his back and the inability to warm up to her in any convincing manner. In the middle of the night he'd wake up screaming and more than once he had his hands around her throat, a gesture he was unable to explain. "He never hit me," she liked to say after their divorce, "but at any moment I thought he might kill me."

I never knew the man my father used to be but my mother says I'm like he was—kind-hearted.

Now he drove in a fury, hands clasped around the steering wheel, eyes scanning the horizon. The movements of other drivers, their accelerations and lane changes, he took as personal affronts. He coasted up to the car ahead, then hit the brakes—a sudden, brief stop. I refused to flinch. In an instant, he changed lanes and floored it.

I chewed the nail on my pinkie and looked out the window. By the side of the road, the wavy green trees gave way to heaps of urban skyline. A neon sign appeared: enormous red lips that lit up in sections, starting at one corner of the mouth and working across, blink, blink, blink, an advertisement for a carpet store. Whenever we drove into the city, I watched for the lips.

My father knew what was about to happen. I still think about this. I'd been told we were on an exploratory mission to the psych ward at Michael Reese Hospital in Chicago, to take a look. But it had already been decided, while I was walking around the house as if nothing was up. Even though my suitcase was in the back, holding my most valued possessions—my cassette player and *The Wall* tape by Pink Floyd—I didn't know I was on my way in, with no way out.

I must have had some inkling, though. With the tall buildings whipping past us on the highway, I made a last-ditch appeal. "Dad, come on," I said. "Don't make me go. I'll be good."

It wasn't until years later—when I'd been in and out, and all the damage had been done—that I asked my father about this drive. We were eating dinner at a restaurant and he looked as handsome as ever; his dark hair was streaked with gray and the back part curled up boyishly. A flirty waitress smiled at him.

"I can't tell you how many times I wanted to turn the car around," he said. But he didn't. "The wheels were in motion," he explained. "It had all been arranged."

At the hospital, my father signed the form. I had just turned fifteen. I didn't think he'd really leave me there. When I was a newborn, I fit in the palm of his hand; at parties, he sat me at the end of his arm to show off my compact self.

My social worker with the pointy high heels had recommended Michael Reese Hospital, after she'd given up on me. She walked without bending her knees, like my sister's Barbie, and my defiance had quickly exhausted her tiny store of curiosity about who I was. "The best adolescent treatment facility around," she'd said.

I didn't let on but part of me kind of wanted to go. Any place had to feel safer than home. Over the summer my father had sat on me, his knees on my shoulders, and poked me in the chest while I tried furiously to kick him, to get him off so I could breathe. He yelled, *Calm down,* and if I could have found my breath I would have screamed, *I am going to suffocate right here on this bed.* I felt his heart pounding above me. His girlfriend observed us from the doorjamb. She had perfect oval nails, painted red; when I was older, she was available to take me for a manicure at a moment's notice. Staring at my father and me wrestling and grunting, she was overcome by agitation and said, "Stop."

After my parents split up, my mother had her own apartment in Rogers Park, on the north side of Chicago, so she didn't know my father was hitting me. Now that she was on her own she wore oversized tee shirts with the names of films written on the front and kept a tin of marijuana on her bedside table. She gave dinner parties with hip people who ate strange food and argued about foreign films; I wanted to have something to say, but all I could do was pick at the tofu curry. She didn't even notice when I walked out of her apartment, ran down the stairs, jumped the wall and crossed the alley into the apartment of Frank, a hairy man who carried a handgun strapped under his arm and another in an ankle holster. Frank told me he was a hit man. At thirteen and fourteen, I didn't know it was possible to say no to a man with a gun who was nice to me besides. One clear memory: the hit man and I are in the bathtub naked. Against my cheek, his chest hair is like bristly fur. I remember his thing as gargantuan but now I think it looked that way because my hand was so small.

I guess if I felt anything riding up the elevator to the third floor of Michael Reese, it was a stab of hope.

THE ATTENDANT in the booth buzzed me in. For a couple of seconds I stood in the entryway to the unit. On either side stretched hallways of beige-flecked linoleum lit by tubes of fluorescent light. In front of me the lounge was jammed with patients who sat three across on a couch and in pairs and alone on pinkish cushy chairs. Almost everyone had cigarettes going, inhaling and exhaling, steering with twitchy hands. Dead air hung over their heads. In between puffs the patients spoke, mostly to themselves—dramatic whispers out the sides of their mouths, snorts of laughter. Two patients, as white-haired as my grandparents, sat in wheelchairs with their heads bent over their knees. In front of them blared a color television. I hadn't expected *old*.

My arrival stirred some head-turning, which caused me to look away. A small-boned man with a scruff of beard dragged himself along a wall. Gravity bore down on him, causing the cuff of his hospital pajama pants to slide over the tops of his sneakers. He pulled a ceramic snake by a curly black telephone cord. The snake was too pink and too green and as he pulled, the snake tipped over, then tipped back and he didn't even notice.

I changed my mind. I turned around and twisted the doorknob to get out but the door was locked behind me.

I had been a bad girl. This I knew, as I waited for the attendant to come get me. As far back as I could remember I'd felt my badness powerfully and felt helpless to redeem myself. Early on my parents had made it clear they would just as soon I go off by myself and not bother them. My mother said that after the age of eight, a child should be on her own. My badness grew, out of boredom. I cut school and stole gold chain necklaces from the religious section of the drugstore. I stole cans of Dinty Moore stew with the Disciples gang and begged for change under the L train so I could buy Mad Dog Twenty-Twenty and swig from the bottle. Pinning me to the ground, the girls at school forced red lipstick onto my mouth and laughed. The social worker with the pointy high heels said I was wrecking the family and that if things kept up the way they were going, with my bad behavior getting all the attention, my parents were going to lose Jean, too.

So, I knew I was bad. I wasn't crazy, though.

I wonder what my parents imagined would happen to me in a mental hospital. They wanted the doctors to tame me but they didn't ask, and the doctors didn't say, exactly what this process entailed. It was the doctors who came up with the idea that I was "an inappropriate female"—that my mouthy ways were a sign of a deep unease in my female nature and that if I learned tips about eyeliner and foundation, I'd be a lot better off. Who would have told my parents this? Not me. Once I was locked up, I lost interest in holding a meaningful conversation with my parents.

I wish they'd known, though. My mother didn't give a rat's ass about whether I wore makeup or girly clothes. My father would have liked me to tie back my hair with a pink barrette, but this wasn't his main concern. He wanted me out of the house before the violence between us exploded.

Still, even if they'd known, I'm not sure it would have made any difference. I don't think they could have stopped the doctors. And in part, my father did wonder if my feminine side was underdeveloped, if this was the source of my rebelliousness. He had his curiosities.

He told me this later. At my last hospital, a counselor asked my father if he had any questions about my treatment.

"Yes," he said. By this time I'd already tried to kill myself, I'd had a guard hold me down with his foot on my head and another patient run his hands over my body as I slept in restraints. Then there was the legacy of my life at home, the way I flinched if someone stood too close.

"Can you tell me," he asked the therapist, "why she won't wear a dress?"

THEY DO THE SEARCH in a small room off the office, after the parent leaves. A clerk went through every pocket of every pair of my torn-up jeans, unrolled the cuffs of my socks, put her hand in the silky lining of my suitcase. I'm certain I had to take off all my clothes down to my bra and underwear to make sure I wasn't hiding a knife or a joint. The strip search also establishes a certain tone: You are the nearly naked patient and we, the clothed, are in charge. I don't remember the strip search.

When she was done, the clerk propped my empty suitcase against the wall. I looked at it fondly and she said, "We keep it." I didn't understand. "Your father can pick it up later," she explained. Of course. Why would I need a suitcase? I had arrived at my destination.

She lifted up my cassette player and studied it. The hospital had a problem with the red Record button. She handed the player over to a mechanic, who unscrewed the bottom of the silver plastic case and, with one quick squeeze of clippers, snipped a wire attached to the microphone. Nothing would be recorded.

DIAGNOSTIC EVALUATION

Referral:

Daphne was referred to Northwest Mental Health Center following an extended evaluation at Doyle Center. That contact extended from 1-26-81 until 5-81 and primarily involved joint interviews with Mrs. S. and Daphne (6), individual interviews with Daphne, Mr. S. and Mrs. S. (1 each) and 6 family interviews. Mrs. S. initially contacted Doyle Center after fights between she and Daphne began escalating. Mrs. S. was concerned about Daphne's stealing, deteriorating school work and truancy. The precipitating event was when Mrs. S. felt provoked to the point where she hit her. . . .

The diagnostic staffing 3-30-81 at Doyle Center concluded that Daphne seemed confused regarding her role in the family and regarding the family structure. She was responding to unclear expectations, responsibilities and rules and was struggling to set up some sort of structure for herself. Her problems seemed to escalate once parents separated. Much of her behavior seemed to be directed at seeking attention and looking for appropriate feedback and limit setting. This same behavior carried over into the school setting. She was seen to carry much of the family's anger and it was speculated that patterns of violence from the parents' families of origin continue through Daphne. There were inconsistencies between the parenting styles of Mr. & Mrs. S. Family therapy was recommended as well as individual therapy for Daphne.

The initial contact at Northwest Mental Health Center was made by Mr. S. upon recommendation of Doyle Center. Another therapist had one individual interview with Daphne and with Mr. S. and felt a referral to ADD (Alcohol and Drug Dependency Program) was appropriate because of Daphne's heavy involvement in drugs and alcohol. Both Mr. S. and ——, social worker at Doyle Center, disagreed and asked that the above stated recommendation be carried out. I then became involved and began an assessment 5-28-81 which led to my recommendation on 6-23-81 for planning a long-term psychiatric hospitalization. During the assessment I was supervised by Dr. —— who concurred and suggested I contact Dr. ——. After sharing my impressions on the phone, he contacted Dr. ——. I have continued to have regular interviews with Daphne and Mr. S. during the Michael Reese evaluation.

——, ACSW

8

T W O

FROM THE BEGINNING, *my mother said*

she needed to find herself, which made no sense since

she was right here with us even if we could tell she

didn't want to be. Though she ate in a delicate

manner in front of us—small bites, neatly

chewed—when I hugged her waist it seemed to be

rounder and rounder. Her walk had a heaviness to

it as she traveled to the counter to make Jean and me peanut butter and jelly and what was the point of living when she was supposed to be an artist but couldn't be?

Her father was an Air Force sergeant and when her family was stationed in upstate New York my mother won the senior class prize for art, even though she was just a sophomore; for her, they made an exception. She loved rolling the ink over the linoleum blocks. Rolling that ink red and blue and black. Art filled her mind with something besides every dreary moment that was her life at home with her father who yelled and drank and told her that because she was the oldest it was her job to keep the house clean and shut up about it.

When I fake-cleaned my room, moving one pile under the bed and another into the closet, she told me that at age eleven she'd put a meal on her family's table every night, a meat, a potato, a vegetable, maybe a dessert but most often not. She said this to show up my shortcomings in the housekeeping department but I could tell that her dinner responsibilities were something she hated about her family, so why would she want me to be tortured, too?

Both of my mother's parents worked and if their Air Force house wasn't kept to her father's liking someone would pay. One night when my mother was twelve, her father dragged her out of bed to hit her around in his drunken state. My grandmother woke up and came into the kitchen to see about the noise and when she saw my mother getting it, she said she didn't need this racket, she had to go to work in the morning. My mother decided right then she was on her own and would never need another soul.

The family was transferred to Tokyo and my mother started her senior year of high school although she was only a junior. A maid was hired to cook the dinners so my mother had spare time. Looking at the pointed-roof Japanese temples gave her happiness. She met my father. He was awfully handsome, pink-cheeked, funny. He strolled into a community theater group for Americans and took notice of my mother, a dark-haired beauty herself. The play was "Black Chiffon" and not much of a drama but they acted the part of a young couple in love and it seemed to happen. "Totally taken with each other"—that's how they were, my mother says. Even after the divorce she'd smile remembering being a high-school girl with an

Army soldier on her arm. She graduated high school early with straight A's, enrolled at Sophia University, a Jesuit school, and thought about all the things a smart girl like her could do in the world. My father was a good dancer, he put his arms around her waist with confidence, then she skipped her period and he didn't want the baby.

My father's Army buddies relayed the information that for forty dollars she could get a Tokyo abortion. My mother didn't think too hard about this since the baby was her way out and she knew it.

The Army chaplain said he knew a home for unwed girls in Louisiana and my mother's father said he'd send her there; she'd give up the baby and be done with it. She said, You send me to America and that will be the last you see of me and the baby and we won't be in Louisiana, either.

My grandfather's Air Force captain had a talk with my father's Army captain. He strongly suggested my father do the right thing. My father got to like the idea of a new baby. So my parents married on Valentine's Day, a touch of romance despite the circumstances. My seventeen-year-old mother was three months along but still slim in a tailored navy blue suit—no white dress for her. The wedding was small and her father wouldn't even go to the Army base chapel. Getting married in Japan was complicated, they had to go to several officials and sign lots of papers, but their marriage became legal on the taxi ride between the United States Embassy and the Japanese Ministry. It was 1966 and before the Army discharged my father they swung him through Vietnam, a short tour which was just long enough to wreck his nature.

THREE

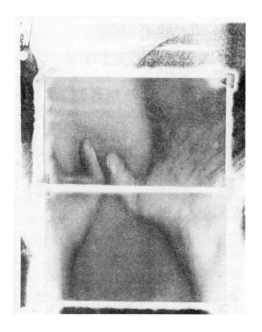

ROOM 304 was pale white. Bed A, my
bed, had white nubby polyester sheets and
a white blanket. A nurse with keys jangling
on her belt wore floor-gripping white
shoes and a white coat like a doctor. I told
her I didn't need to be here. "Uh-huh," she
said. I told her my parents were divorced
and my sister needed me at home very

much and my father had a lot of problems. My mother, too. She said, "Hold out your arm."

"No needles," I said, and she said, "Just a pulse." She grabbed my wrist with unnecessary force and wrote my pulse in my chart on a clipboard. Same with my temperature. I could see she was going to write down everything so I told her my boyfriend was killed by the police on his birthday and died in my arms, blood everywhere, but there was nothing I could do to save him.

"Oh really?" she said. She looked at me with concern. I said, "Yeah," and shrugged as if it were no big deal.

Later, through the door at the nurses' station that split—top-half open, bottom-half closed—I told her, "When I get out of here, I'm going to be a rock musician. It's all set up. I've got a contract."

"Oh really?" she said.

I mentioned that I was lucky to be alive considering that when I was twelve a car hit me and broke both my legs and my right arm, fractured my pelvis and my skull and I had to lie in traction.

"Oh?" she said.

When my mother visited, she told the nurses I had an active imagination.

Lies: I told them for the flash of concern on the nurse's face, the look of interest. What I really meant, what I wanted to say, I couldn't find the words for.

MY SECOND DAY in I met my psychiatrist, Dr. Browning. We were supposed to meet at 10 a.m. but 10 a.m. came and went and he breezed onto the unit in his white coat and black shoes at 10:25, no explanation, never mind an apology. It was understood that I was free all the time and that whenever he cared to arrive I'd sit in a room and tell him my deepest feelings. So we did not get off to a good start and I was not inclined to like doctors in the first place, since they acted superior. When I grew bolder, I delivered the greeting a lot of patients gave their doctors: "Well, if it isn't Dr. Sigmund Fraud."

On the hallway, one side was double rooms, the other side was singles and some of these had been left mostly bare so they could be offices. We entered one. Two chairs with cushions on the back beside a coffee table; I think it was old furniture from the lounge.

Dr. Browning had wire-rimmed glasses which made his dark eyes look bigger than they were. I looked at his eyes but he did not look at mine; if he caught my glance, he turned away and I knew that to him I was a specimen, a thing he was studying.

We sat down. He crossed his left knee over his right and adjusted his yellow legal pad so it balanced on his left thigh. All settled in, he asked, "Do you know why you're here, Daphne?"

Why should I make it easy for him? Besides, I wanted to hear him explain me to me. "No." He started in about my problems at school, cutting class, miserable grades, threatening a teacher. He said I was failing school and a thought popped up, How come no one ever says school is failing me? I didn't say this. He continued peering at me through his wire-rimmed glasses. I had a problem with authority figures, he said, and I thought, Okay, this is cool, I can admit to this. I said, Yeah, yeah, I know.

He asked me about problems at home and I told him my father hit me, my mother doesn't want me around, and he scribbled away, flipping up pages as he went. We moved along to drugs and alcohol and I exaggerated my use because doctors always like to hear about youth and drugs.

His pen paused in its scratching and I thought I could throw him a question for a change. I asked him what my diagnosis was. I knew this was a major deal; it was like being a Disciple or a Latin King; it was your identity in the hospital; when the doctor looked at you, he didn't see you, he saw *paranoid* or *schizophrenic.*

Dr. Browning said I had a multiple diagnosis because of the complexity of my situation. I liked the sound of that: the complexity of my situation. One of the diagnoses was Conduct Disorder, which made sense to me, I've never been one to lie about my bad behavior. He said another diagnosis was Mixed Substance Abuse, which I knew to be a stretch of the truth but what did I care if he thought I had a drug problem.

He rolled his pen between his fingers for a moment. He said the other diagnosis was something called Gender Identity Disorder, which he said I'd had since Grade 3, according to my records. He said what this means is you are not an appropriate female, you don't act the way a female is supposed to act.

I looked at him. I didn't mind being called a delinquent, a truant, a hard kid who smoked and drank and ran around with a knife in her sock. But I didn't want to be called something I wasn't. Gender screw-up or whatever wasn't cool. My foot started to jiggle, I couldn't stop it. He was calling me a freak, not normal. He was like the boys in Little League calling out tomboy, tomboy, and Michelle who pinned me down for the red lipstick treatment. He was like the boys who yelled, *Let me see your titties,* when I rode shirtless on my bike in the wind.

Actually, Dr. Browning was worse. He had an official name for me.

He was saying that every mean thing that had happened to me was my fault because I had this gender thing. I knew I walked tough and sat with my legs apart and did not defer to men and boys, but I was a girl in the only way I knew how to be one.

He clicked his pen and slipped it in the pocket of his white coat. I knew the matter was settled, that nothing would make him change his mind. Anything I said now would be written in my chart as *defensive behavior.*

Michael Reese Hospital & Medical Center
Date: 9/11 Fellow's Admission Note

1st psychiatric admission for this 14 1/2 year old SWF brought by both parents after referral from outside MHC. History obtained from parents, patient, past evaluation records. Presenting Problems include:

1. Violent Behavior @ home and a pattern of abusive behavior towards authority figures.
2. Multiple drug use.
3. School failure and multiple school suspensions and expulsion from a Chicago High School.

4. Family problems, parents separated and unable to establish secure, consistent provision of home for child.

History is very long and complicated and the problems which led to hospitalization basically began 3 yrs ago, with parents' separation. Since then there has been an escalation of pt's behavioral acting out with the above problems becoming evident. During past year there have been two episodes of violent behavior in mother's home, school failure and a problem of shoplifting and petty stealing. Heavy use of multiple drugs is noted by both parents and admitted by patient.

Past history of development milestones is unremarkable. A Gender Identity Disorder has been present since Grade 3. The patient has been in various treatments since Grade 3 as well. There is no family history of psychiatric illness.

No major medical problems are noted.

Mental Status: frightened, anxious young woman appearing her stated age, who although dressed as a tomboy was sexually provocative.

No thought disorder noted.

Rate, rhythm, conduct of speech, normal.

Affect depressed, frightened, consistent with conduct of thought.

Impression: Patient's behavior has been out of control for some time now and parents have been unable to establish limit setting. There are severe psycho social stressors with parents' separation and apparent emotional abandonment of child. She seems to be an unhappy, frightened girl who has a great deal of secondary depressive affect, primitive rage, a permissive superego and grandiose expectations. I like her, however, and she has several strengths.

Initial diagnosis:

1. Conduct disorder, Socialized, Unaggressive vs. Identity Disorder (Borderline Disorder of Childhood)

17

2. Gender Identity Disorder
3. Mixed Substance Abuse.
Initial Treatment Plan filled out.

—————, M.D.

TIME TURNED SOLID, like a wall. Who knew what time it was? I never saw a patient wearing a watch. One clock was at the nurses' station, to keep track of shifts, the other was in the lounge so we'd know when our tv shows were coming on. Afternoons we watched *All My Children, One Life to Live, General Hospital,* one soap opera slopped into the next. We'd turn the channel if the news appeared; we never saw newspapers. The first term of the Reagan administration passed while I was locked up. The only thing I knew about Reagan was that his economic plan was to blame if we ran out of Styrofoam cups or if we didn't have enough staff to do an activity.

Outside, time mattered. Inside we didn't want to know how much time was passing us by. We knew it was going slowly, but it was going. In seclusion, especially, time was a wall that closed in; we scratched at it with a plastic spoon.

On 3 East and West, the older people were the scariest; they were us if we weren't careful. We called Margaret "the incredible shrinking woman" because her wheelchair swallowed her up. Someone walking by would say, "My, Margaret, you're looking smaller today," and she'd raise her head and scowl. We'd have these one-way conversations with her. She'd pee and shit in her chair and when an attendant came to clean her, she'd let loose with "No contact! No contact!" She sat in her shit for hours. The smell was subtle at first. We'd sniff and think, what's that smell? It grew stronger until it gagged you. She was the oldest, so she was entitled.

Daytime the older ones parked in front of the television; you could walk right up and turn the channel and no one would make a peep.

Even the younger ones looked old, if they had the big-time diagnoses: paranoid schizophrenia or manic depression. Pacing and screaming, they'd worn themselves out.

Bob was twenty-two and busy. He paced the halls so hard his tee shirt had sweat-rings under the arms.

"Hi, Bob," I said.

"I am Jesus," he said. "I know it's hard to believe, but I am Jesus."

A couple of times I paced with him, down the long corridor and back, for exercise. As we turned the corner he asked, "Have you accepted me as your savior?" He wasn't mean about it. Just curious.

I wanted to help him. I was always this way, helping my friends. I thought of myself as a roving counselor. It kept people a nice distance away from my problems. Being in the mental hospital was a boon for my counseling skills, although after a while I got confused. For instance, the more I talked to Jesus, the more I liked him, and the less crazy he seemed. Zealous, but not dangerous. I could imagine him in the outside world, preaching. He'd probably help some people.

This posed an interesting dilemma: If I thought he was sane, what did that make me? Mental hospitals are rife with this kind of debate. Are people like Bob simply more sensitive than the rest of us? Bombarded with information, the delusional find it hard to function in the world, but is that their fault or the world's? The staff discouraged this sort of questioning. They liked the line between sane and insane to be perfectly clear.

"I used to hear voices," I told Jesus. This wasn't true, but I didn't want him to feel alone. Plus, I wanted to fit in. "I've come to realize they have no power over me. They're just voices, Bob."

"Hmm," he said, considering this. He wasn't convinced but my interest made us friends. He told me his visions—what he and John the Baptist had been up to. Listening to him was like going to the movies, without the pictures; it was a great distraction. He said the twelve apostles were in the area. I asked, "So have they gotten in touch with you?" and he said he hadn't heard from them in a while but they had a plan. They were going to have a reunion at a bar on Rush Street in Chicago.

Bob took anti-psychotic meds mixed with orange juice in a tiny plastic cup. He let me have a sip but it tasted gross.

The other famous person in the unit was Jimi. I asked him, "What's your name?" and he said, "Jimi." That's all I knew about him for a while. Another patient told me that it was Jimi as in Jimi Hendrix. He was white, twenty-five years old, with a wispy brown mustache. I didn't like him as much as Jesus, maybe because I took music more seriously than religion. In music therapy, Jimi was confronted with a guitar. He picked it up and strummed a few lame notes, his eyes closed, his fingers fluttering.

"Don't you know you're dead?" I asked him.

"Am not," he said. He cocked his head and listened to music that was entirely different from the noise we heard.

Jimi could seem totally normal. We'd be in the lounge having a regular conversation about the nurses and he'd say, This is just like what happened at one of my concerts. And I'd think, What? And then, Whoa.

None of the crazy people knew they were insane. I'd sit around thinking, I am so sane in comparison to these folks, and then a flicker of a thought would reach my brain. Maybe I don't know I'm insane. They don't know they're insane, so why should I know? Maybe I don't realize I'm walking around saying I'm Patsy Cline.

At this point I liked to go to my room, turn on my cassette player and listen to music so loud I'd max out the volume and make the machine vibrate.

CHOOSING OUR MEALS for the next day became a time-consuming activity. We sat on the cushy seats in the lounge and studied the piece of folded white paper that came up from the cafeteria. The words on the menu were fuzzy, as if they'd been typed on a very old typewriter, and next to each word—French toast, Jell-O, meatloaf—was a dash for us to check off.

The anorexics, Julie and Lisa, spent at least an hour huddling over their menus, adding up the calories. Snooty—that was Julie, with her cheekbones sticking out. If she liked you, she gave you a glossy black-and-white photo of her face with her name on the bottom—her modeling headshot. Fifteen, with her nose in *Cosmopolitan*. Pen in hand, she filled out the *Cosmo* questionnaires diligently. *Your romance I.Q.* If she licked a stamp, she counted the glue in her required daily calorie intake.

Lisa spoke with a British accent, I don't know where she was from, but it was a real accent. Instead of saying butt, she said bum. She pulled at her thighs—there was nothing there but bones. She said, "Yuck." I thought, If you get any thinner, when I exhale I'm going to blow you across the room. In front of the nurse she said, "I'm going to have to put on some weight." Actors, all of us. When we horsed around, sat on each other's laps in the lounge, Lisa's tailbone was like a dagger.

With lunch or dinner we could order one can of soda. Every once in a while, I'd order two cans of Mountain Dew, and sometimes they'd appear on my tray when the nurse pulled it out of the metal rack. I imagined a worker down in the kitchen saying, Oh, okay.

I never drank my soda. By the time the staff at Michael Reese ordered me transferred to another hospital, I must have had two hundred cans of it in my bathroom cabinet. Stacked-up cans in neat rows: it was comforting to look at them. I'd use the soda to trade for a deck of cards, or cigarettes. I'd keep track of inventory. I'd think, I'm running low on Tab and I know Julie likes Tab and someone brought her a box of candy, which she'll never eat, so I'll order up a Tab and trade.

When the hospital transferred me out, the staff never gave me my soda. I spent a long time collecting that soda and I could have taken it to the next hospital and used it for leverage.

When we were bored, somebody might go up to the nurses' station and ask for the green volume of the *Diagnostic and Statistical Manual of Mental Disorders*, third edition. The nurse would hand it through the split door—she didn't care if you borrowed it. Somebody would page through it on the couch and a couple of us would come around, just the younger patients, and ask, "Hey, would you look up paranoid schizophrenic?" The person holding the book would look that up and we'd read from the manual. Then we'd flip to the last entry in the book, zoophilia. Sex with animals, *ha ha*. Someone would ask, "What are you in for?" We looked up anorexia for Julie and Lisa. Manic depression? Borderline personality? Obsessive-compulsive? I didn't tell anyone about my gender thing. I said I was in for Conduct Disorder.

We placed bets that we could get a new diagnosis added on. No money, just a dare.

Danny was a Disciples gang member but from a different part of Chicago, so I'd never known him. His voice was pure. Handsome, the only black teenage boy on the unit. He sang "Precious Blood" and then slid into a Luther Vandross number. In the hallway, he taught us how to break-dance; on the linoleum, we spun around on our butts—our bums, as Lisa put it. Out-of-control behavior was what Danny was in for—or maybe his parents just wanted him out of the gang. He always seemed fine to me.

He bet he could get hallucinations written on his chart. This was tricky. It had to be convincing, so he started out small. "Did you hear that?" he asked, and we shook our heads, no.

Heather was the rich girl on the unit, tight Guess jeans and a pink Izod polo shirt. Super bratty. Baby fat in her cheeks, blond hair she sucked in her mouth. I don't know why she was in, I guess her parents couldn't handle her or maybe she'd tried suicide. Her first day on the unit, her old boyfriend brought her a stuffed brown bull with white horns and a black nose. Big animal, three feet high, a couple of feet long, a foot wide. The next morning I snuck into her room and threw the bull on her bed where she was sleeping. She roared out of the room saying, "Who did this?" I was back in my room, la, la, la, all innocent. The housekeeper told on me. After a while Heather thought it was funny so we were best friends.

She looked the way my doctors wanted me to look, smooth and girly. I asked my father and his girlfriend to send me Izod shirts and button-down collars, like hers. Mostly I wore jeans and tee shirts that said Led Zeppelin or Pink Floyd, nice and ratty.

"Why do you wear clothes like that?" Columbia, the attendant, asked me.

Even in her white nurse pants, Columbia looked hip. "It's such a shame," she said. "You could fix yourself up to look pretty."

Everything she said made me feel ugly. I said, "Whatever."

Heather decided to go for split personalities. She had a role model in Anne, who lived downstairs where security was higher. Anne was a legend. First thing on the unit, you heard this muffled screaming from downstairs: that was Anne. She had eight personalities. Columbia said Anne had attacked an attendant, hurt him, and she'd attacked patients, too, with her bare hands. Anne's screaming grew loud like the 'L' train rumbling by when we took the elevator down to the activities room. When Danny pinched Heather's butt in the elevator, Columbia said, "You don't want to go live with Anne, do you?" She wasn't kidding.

Heather figured split personalities was a snap. One second she was her usual spoiled, be-bop self, demanding, "Give me my diet Sprite," and the next—after a few transitional moments—she was a mewling three-year-old with her thumb in her mouth.

I bet I could get anorexia written on my chart. The anorexics were psyched. The more anorexics, the better—the less attention anyone would be paying to what they weren't eating.

First thing to do to fake anorexia was to stand at dinner, one foot jiggling. I knew this from Julie and Lisa. We ate, and jiggled, and talked about the negative calories in chewing lettuce. They told me how many calories were in each forkful of broccoli.

I arranged my face in an expression of fascination. "Really?" I said.

I watched what food Julie and Lisa left behind on their plates and tried to leave a little bit more.

"Did you hear that?" Danny asked. He ran up to a nurse's aide. "Did you hear that?" He ran into his room and huddled on his bed, like he was really scared.

Heather put her thumb in her mouth. "Mommy," she said. The nurse's aide gave her a glance.

In therapy, Dr. Browning asked me, "Are you not feeling well?"

I said, "I think I'm fat." And I knew *tendencies toward anorexia* had made it onto my chart.

Danny quit the hallucinations after a while. You didn't want to go too far with that, or you'd end up swallowing a cupful of medication that might be more than you'd bargained for.

Heather grew tired of being a three-year-old. She shifted out of being three gradually, so the nurses would be on edge, waiting for the other personality to come back.

Even if we'd looked up Gender Identity Disorder, I don't think anyone would have tried to fake it. We knew the rules: pacing, screaming, hallucinating and vomiting were okay. Not okay was walking around with a scarf in your hair, for a boy, or being like me, a girl who never felt comfortable in a dress.

F O U R

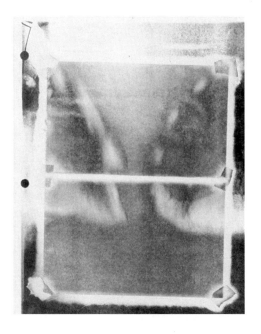

AS A BOY *in Janesville, Wisconsin, my father*
thought his future was being an actor or studying at
the Lutheran seminary in a long black robe. In the
meantime, instead of waiting for the draft, he signed
up for the Army——but only after they promised
him he wouldn't have to fire a gun. They put
him in intelligence. Nothing was written down.

Someone would tell him something and he'd go someplace and tell someone else.

He was in the wet green fields of Vietnam with gunfire going off so close that sleep was shallow and full of dreams that made his feet jerk around; his sweat dampened the sheets. A grenade flew into the bunker and exploded. Blood splattered on my father's skin and when he looked up, he saw the soldier beside him limp and wrecked and dead. He bolted outside. Another grenade burst and threw him against a wall. The impact broke his back. He rolled into a trench and lay there until the gunner who was on the wall above him fell to the ground, shot dead.

My father climbed up, broken back and all, not feeling the pain one speck, and took over for the gunner because now it was up to him to protect himself. Even though he didn't want to fire a gun and kill people he held onto the machine gun and fired away. By the time the shooting was done, part of him was done, too. My mother said the fear had sent him someplace awful and the only sign of what had happened to him was a terrible anger. My father said he was fine, the war was in the past.

A helicopter took him to a hospital where doctors put a pin in his spine to stabilize it and operated on his arms and back. They found shrapnel everywhere, bitty pieces. With pin-sharp tweezers they plucked out what they could but even now my father has metal working its way to the surface of his skin, looking for a way out.

While my father was in the Army hospital in Japan, my pregnant mother moved to Wisconsin to meet the in-laws and start her new life, away from her father with the quick fists who demanded dinner on the table every night. Being far from her parents' house was divine—she wasn't a teenager anymore, she was a wife. Her in-laws hugged her and said they loved her, which made my mother suspicious. She says she didn't know how to love anyone until her children were born.

When my father returned there was no talk of being a pastor now. He studied architecture, which was a comfort to him in its orderliness. At home he liked everything just so. He wasn't funny anymore and wouldn't say a word to my mother or his parents or anyone about Vietnam so stop asking. Only after their marriage was dead did he talk about it with a psychiatrist at my hospital. He said he wasn't depressed, his wife was wrong, it was fear he felt when he remembered how the killing rage had surged through his body like a current. It could come back at any time if he wasn't careful. At home he'd get an empty look on his face and tell me that when bullets fly, they scream. I thought about this for a long time.

My father reported for Army duty in Northern California, where I was born, then pretty soon we moved to Wisconsin to be near my grandparents. My mother grew glum and fed up with taking care of me. One day when I was a squirmy baby she held me in her arms on the bus going over a bridge. Looking at the rail and the shiny water below, she thought, I could just throw her off the bridge. She told me this just recently. I said, "Oh, really," as if I didn't care.

My father took charge of the bottle-feeding. He said we had the best time, the two of us. As soon as I could walk and gurgle a few words I'd rush the door when he came home and he'd swoop me up and make me fly.

My grandmother was a cook at a nursing home and made soupy, goulashy things. When I was older Grandma would take me to work and I'd cruise the nursing home, stopping into people's rooms where they were always happy to have me come in and sit on the bed and talk. I was in demand and didn't mind the smells.

At the University of Wisconsin my mother studied art, she wasn't going to let her mind rot, she had to plan for the future. She didn't want to be in a trap, which seemed to be us. Making prints my mother lost track of time, of people, of everything but her own thoughts and the ink on her hands. At home she walked around and imagined colors and shapes. My father said she had to give it up, he needed her and so did the baby. She loved the art more than she loved him and this was trouble so she gave up the art and started to hate my father a bit, underneath. My parents moved to a crummy apartment and my mother told my social worker, years later, that she'd never loved my father but she'd married him because she thought he'd be a good family man. Well, that will only take you so far and it ran out early.

She went into business, managing a hearing-aid service, and she brought home money and was happy, sort of. She'd smile, fussing over her geraniums on the front porch, pinching off the brown leaves and testing the soil for dampness with her forefinger, but all the while wanting to be someplace else.

My sister Jean came along when I was three going on four and from the minute I saw her squished-up baby face I knew I had to save her.

THE JOBS WERE BETTER in Chicago so we moved to Lombard, Illinois, where we lived in a tall apartment building with a swatch of grass in the courtyard. An old lady invited me up to her apartment for tea and my mother said, I'd better come with you, but after the first time she let me go by myself. The old lady poured me tea in a cup just like a grown-up and I could tell she liked me because she invited me back. I wondered if she could be my mother or if she were too old. Everywhere we went, I looked for a family to take me in.

Pretty soon we moved to Roselle, where we had a townhouse with a hill out back for sledding. I'd gone to kindergarten in the Montessori style, where they let me draw and paint and roam around the class and do what I wanted, so first grade at Schaumburg Elementary was a shock. Mrs. B told me to sit in my chair and quit drifting around the room. I discovered restlessness in school and it was an awful thing to know. I wanted to skip ahead in the book but Mrs. B told me to keep quiet and follow along the page everyone else was on.

I don't know what happened—I started not to feel things. In second grade I stopped raising my hand and when the teacher said, "Daphne, how do you spell banana," I pretended I didn't hear. It didn't occur to me that she truly cared to listen to my answer.

My teacher called me up to her desk and said, "Why don't you talk?" She said it kind of mean. "Say something," she said. "Don't you feel anything?" I slid my fingertip into the black stapler on her desk and pushed down. The staple went into the cushy side of my finger like a pinprick. It didn't really hurt. She looked at me as if I were whacked.

By the time I was in third grade my mother was trying to decide whether to kill herself. I found out later that she was running exact plans through her mind. She didn't have to say the words for me to know—her face was permanently sad; the sadness made her mind wander off even when she looked right at me. The eerie quiet of the house slipped inside me. At school I drew a picture of myself hanging from the moon, my fingers edging over the tip of the crescent. I dreamed I was flying and Mom, Dad, Jean, Charcoal the cat and Pudgy the dog were dots I couldn't even see, I was so high up.

When I didn't have my homework done my third-grade teacher, Miss Martin, said, "I'm going to have to hang you by your toes," but she hugged me so I knew she wasn't going to hang me. I wanted to run home and do my homework double-quick, but when I walked through the front door I couldn't think. Worry made my brain feel full. Two mothers of kids in my classroom died that year, a strange thing, and I wondered when I was going to walk into the house and find my mother dead because it was going around.

At night I called Miss Martin on the telephone in the kitchen. I was in my pjs and lonely even though Jean was right next to me in the trundle that pulled out from under my bed. I made up a question about my homework which Miss Martin knew I wasn't going to do anyway. In a soothing voice she said, "Now go right back to bed and tuck yourself in and dream sweet dreams." I felt better once she said that.

In bed I lay on my side and rocked back and forth, back and forth, until I fell asleep, still rocking. From her bed six inches away Jean said, "Quit it." Softly at first and then louder. "Quit it, quit it," she said and I woke up but pretended to sleep so I could keep rocking. She kneeled up in her bed and put her hands on my shoulders. "Quit it," she said, and I kept my eyes closed. "Quit it, quit it," she said, and I giggled, and grabbed her hands and wrestled her, which got her giggling, too.

After we settled down in our beds, Charcoal crept in and situated herself between my feet and I could sleep then without rocking, listening to her motor purr.

IN CLASS. Miss Martin read to us and I sat up close on the floor and petted her leg. She wore long pants and she'd let a bunch of us pet her leg and I was always right in front, petting. We'd peek to see her special socks—jack-o'-lanterns, snowmen, polka dots.

Miss Martin said I was a sad child and why wasn't my mother paying attention? She sent me to the school counselor, Mrs. Stein, which was all right because I got to skip class and we played games together. Her favorite was *The Career Game*. She held up cards with pictures of a policeman, a farmer, a construction worker, a secretary and a nurse, and I said which ones I'd like to be: police officer and construction worker. She looked at me with a curious face like a mother robin. She was the first one who said I had a problem with my gender. I didn't know what that meant, but later I found out she thought I wanted to be a boy. I didn't really know if I wanted to be a boy, but I wanted to go shirtless outside in summer and play rough. I could hit the ball harder than the boys, anyway, so why would I want to be one?

I wore tee shirts and hooded sweatshirts, pants, sneakers. When I was little my mother dressed me in a frilly dress and combed my hair back tight along my scalp into a bun. I squinted from the hair-pulling pain. My dress was immaculate and stiff. I waited for the snap of the camera button, so I could take off my dress and be myself again.

I was eight, nine, ten and my parents let me pick out what I wanted to wear although sometimes my father would say, "Don't you want to wear a dress?" If I ever did wear a lacy white number I'd be flooded with remarks—"Oooh, you look so pretty today"—which were meant to inspire me but didn't. I wasn't concerned with being pretty. I wanted to be free to run.

FIVE

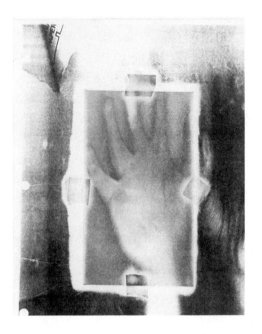

Michael Reese Hospital & Medical Center
Institute for Psychosomatic and
Psychiatric Research and Training
Psychiatric Progress Notes
9-17-81 (8-4:30) 4 p.m.
Daphne presents a tomboyish appearance
with jeans, T-shirt and a manner of
relating which is not entirely feminine.
However, she is intelligent & very
sensitive to other people on the unit.
                              ——, R.N.

IT WAS SEPTEMBER but school in the mental hospital hadn't started yet so we sat in the lounge and played Spades, which is like Hearts. Four people played in teams, two against two. Danny and I were partners, bidding, faking out the other team. When she was in a good mood, Columbia played. We always needed somebody to sit in because we played to five hundred points and it took hours. Laughing and playing, killing time.

Across the room we'd hear patients playing Sorry, a board game. Every few minutes, one would say, "Sorry." Then another, "Sorry." "Sorry."

When we weren't playing Spades, I took a cigarette and flipped it in the air to try to get it to land in my mouth, so it would hang from my lip, looking cool. Danny tried it, Julie, Lisa, Heather. Almost everyone smoked.

I had another trick. I could turn my Styrofoam coffee cup inside out. It was possible, if you took it slow. I was proud of this.

In between we had therapy—group plus sessions with our own doctors. Before Dr. Browning saw me, he'd read about my behavior in the nurses' chart. Now he'd rephrase everything. "You've been angry, lately," he'd say. "Acting out."

There was no right answer to this statement. He made everything sound suspicious.

On another day, he'd say, "You've been quiet. Depressed."

If the nurses had written that I'd been pacing, he'd say I was "hyperactive." If I'd been sitting around a lot, I was "withdrawn." If I said I needed help, I was "looking for attention." If I said I didn't need help, I was "in denial."

I did my best to fend him off. He'd say, Don't you want to clean yourself up? And I'd say, I took a shower this morning. He meant my jeans with the white threads showing in the thigh and couldn't I wear something that wasn't so ragged?

Once a week we had a unit meeting. Everyone sat in a circle in the lounge, Jesus, Jimi Hendrix, all the older people, everyone. During one week Columbia had sassed us out. She could be mean for no reason, treating us like idiots. She loved to call security to shush us up and they could be rough. This time they went after Jesus because he wouldn't go into his room at bedtime. He kept pacing. Three guards held him down on the floor and Jesus whipped his body around, screaming and crying. The guards swore at him. It was nasty. So what if Jesus wouldn't go into his room? He was peaceful until they arrived. Another patient, I don't remember who, ran over with me to help Jesus. We yelled, Leave him alone, he's not hurting anyone. A guard with huge arms wrestled me to the floor and put his black leather boot on my head. He stood over me for a long moment to make sure I understood who held the power. I understood. "Shut up, you fucking crazy-ass queer," he said. The next day my neck and shoulder were so sore the nurse gave me Tylenol.

In the meeting we didn't mention Jesus being beaten up. We complained about Columbia being a control freak, not letting us watch television, and the head nurse nodded and did nothing. So the next day we made a plan. Danny and I were the leaders. We called it *the riot*. At two o'clock in the afternoon the nurses had reports in the nursing station so five or six of us circled the station and taped the windows with notes that said "Fuck You." We taped the notes so they could read the "Fuck You" part from the inside. Pushing two lounge tables against the door, we barricaded the nurses, but eventually they escaped.

We sat on the couch, la, la, la, knowing nothing about it. In her wheelchair, Margaret twisted around to see what was up, aggravated by all the activity. She sat there swearing. An attendant told her to shut up.

Punishment came down swiftly. Everyone was restricted to the unit, no tv, no activities, but it blew over.

Arts and crafts we had downstairs in the basement. In silversmithing, I held a blowtorch in my hand and thought, God, I'm okay with this torch but do they let every nut in the place use it? Danny melted down some gold from somewhere and made beautiful rings, like Cartier, three bands of different colors of gold that rolled on your finger.

Michael Reese Hospital & Medical Center
Institute for Psychosomatic and Psychiatric Research and Training
Psychiatric Progress Notes
9-15-81 (8-4:00)

Appeared depressed. Much time to self. While talking w. writer became tearful & reported feeling depressed & abandoned. Mother didn't show for 3rd time. Father lied about trying to call her. (She never got a call from him.) Cannot contact sister & is worried. Said she hasn't eaten today ("no appetite") & has lost 5 lbs. Asked writer to help fill out menu. Said she wanted some mothercare.

—, R.N.

Michael Reese Hospital & Medical Center
Institute for Psychosomatic and Psychiatric Research and Training
Daily staff report 9/27/81 (8-4:00) 3:00
Continued talking about friends in gangs & peer drug involvement. Insisted that she would not accept drugs from friends if they visited. However, spoke of missing drugs and alcohol. Continued discussion re: wanting to learn to cry and express emotions. Spoke of emotionless home, of wanting mothering and tenderness, of wishing she could be adopted by writer.

—, R.N.

"I won't take up much room," I told the nurse. She wore a white skirt and blouse and thick-soled nurses' shoes and her name was Kay. She was my favorite. She came into my room and rubbed my shoulders while I sat in a chair doing nothing. "I don't eat much," I said. "One meal a day is fine."

I wanted her to be my mother. *Adopted* was a word I turned around in my mind. My parents would be glad to see me go. Jean, well, Jean I couldn't save.

Kay said it wouldn't be possible. She said it nicely so I wouldn't take offense. She was sweet to me, always a big hug hello. Mostly I'd lost the ability to cry but I could cry with Kay, a split-second rush of tears.

In my hospital chart, my therapist wrote: *Patient has no sense of home.*

On the unit, when we talked about home, it wasn't the home we'd come from. It was the home we were going to. Hawaii, maybe, to go surfing, or a penthouse apartment where we'd have our friends over and drink frozen strawberry daiquiris. We were going to live in houses with velour couches in rich neighborhoods, like the people we saw on *All My Children*.

Danny said the first thing he'd do when he got out was get laid. The guys always said that. Heather made plans to go directly to *The Rocky Horror Picture Show*. I planned to go with her. Anywhere sounded good to me.

One of the new girls, a shy one with disheveled hair, said, "My mother doesn't know I'm here. As soon as she finds out, she's going to come get me. I'm not going to be here long."

We felt sorry for her.

Downstairs, one of the really bad anorexics was going home because her insurance was running out. Her eyes looked huge in their bony sockets, so the doctors hurried up and gave her shock treatment to blast away her fear of food. Six months later, she walked onto the unit to see the doctors, thin as paper. After a while, we heard she was dead.

Real home we almost never mentioned. A couple of times I tried to tell the counselors about Mahmoud, my mother's violent boyfriend. Mahmoud was from Iraq and had the widest back. He'd have to turn sideways to pass me in the hall. He made us babaganouj, Middle Eastern stuff. My mother said he was a scholar, she admired his mind.

Mahmoud beat his daughter with a broom so the straw part lashed her legs. He didn't touch my sister and me except that when I'd leave the apartment he'd throw ashtrays out the window at me. I'd stop and pick them up from the grass. They were the heavy, square, glass ashtrays people used to have; I'd put them in my backpack and bring them home afterward. They weren't his ashtrays to be throwing around.

When I called home from the hospital Mahmoud said he was going to take my mother to Iraq and I would never see her again and if she didn't go he was going to kill her. I told the staff, This guy is threatening to kill my family. I was worried Mahmoud was going to come and kill me. My counselor wrote in my chart *paranoid thinking*.

In the first few weeks I was locked up, Mahmoud did try to kill my mother. He cornered her in the living room and told his daughter to get a butcher knife from the kitchen. My mother begged him to let her go and he tore her blouse with his hands, rip, rip, and her pants and everything until she was naked except for her shoes. With some shred of charm she calmed him for a moment.

Grabbing a coat for my mother and my mother's purse, Jean ran to the door and my mother broke away. They fled through the park, my mother naked under her coat, freezing. She called the police.

I thought, Wow, I must be really screwed up because this guy is free. Sure, there's a restraining order, but nobody's taking him away. Nobody's locking him up.

Eventually Mahmoud flew to Saudi Arabia where he was immediately deported for being the wrong kind of Muslim. They put him on a plane back to America and he couldn't stand the idea so he held a plastic dinner knife to the stewardess's throat and tried to hijack the plane to London. The pilot wouldn't stop. I understand why the stewardess believed he could kill her with just a plastic knife. He could do it. My mother found out about the hijacking because she saw his picture in the paper. Probation was all he got.

On the unit, I knew the routine and sometimes it was peaceful and once in a while it felt like home. A few months after I was admitted, a woman in her mid-thirties arrived, a sad and loving person. Super depressed. She had a five-year-old boy and she was lonely for her child. With her cushy, padded body, I could tell she'd be a cozy mother to be small next to. She wasn't allowed off the unit and, because of his age, her son wasn't allowed on. The only option to see him was to cooperate and get a pass so she could go down to the lobby. When I was on suicide precautions and they let me sleep in the lounge instead of my room—which I preferred, because then nobody could sneak into my room and start rambling—this woman stayed up with me.

Sliding six pieces of modular furniture together, I made a rectangle with sides all around it, like a crib. I lay down in the middle and stared at the ceiling and she looked in on me. "You want a story?" she asked. " 'Jack and the Beanstalk'? 'Three Bears'?" They all were new to me.

"Once there was a little, bitty bear," she said. "A wee bear who lived in a cottage." Her face was round like a moon above me.

I can't remember her name. She didn't stay long. A lot of people came and went.

We entertained ourselves in the lounge after dinner, waiting for the nurse to come out with a tray of medication in little cups. She'd circulate like a waitress at a cocktail party—a sedative for you, an anti-psychotic for you. For me, an orange and yellow Dalmane capsule, a sleeping pill that conked me out all night and into the day.

Danny turned a chair around and pretended to be driving a car. Jimi Hendrix pulled his chair around to be up front in the passenger seat, riding along like the famous person he was. Jesus and I were already sitting beside each other on the couch so we were in the backseat. Jesus waved to the nurse as we drove.

I said, "Hey, is that Jack in the Box up there? Can we stop? Because I'd really like a cheeseburger."

Jesus said, "Yeah, I could go for some fries."

Danny said, "Not right now."

So we kept driving like any other family on the highway, traveling together.

NURSE KAY got assigned to another unit temporarily so I wrote her a letter. Copying the words to "Just the Way You Are" by Billy Joel, I explained this was exactly how I felt about her.

. . . I don't know what, but you remind me of a perfect mother, something I have wished for my entire life. You make me happy and you are kind and giving and you are able to love and care for someone. That is something my parents have never been able to

do. Also you have feeling and you allow people to have feelings. My parents were never able to do that either. One more thing, you can make me smile, even if I'm in the worst mood. In other words I am still asking or wondering if you will adopt me. You make me so happy and I know I could make you happy.

The doctors read this letter and all the others I wrote to her.

PRETTY QUICKLY, I got my first marriage proposal. Mental hospitals are packed with would-be grooms, ardent and devoted.

Arthur and I met at volleyball, which we played in the basement of the hospital. Everyone who wasn't in a wheelchair played—the psychotics, the schizophrenics, the anorexics, the depressives. Arthur had a lot of energy for someone who was in for suicidal tendencies. He ran around like a person on speed. Jesus, too, was a maniac with the ball. The thing about playing in the basement was the ceiling was way too low. The ball would shoot up and hit the tiles, then blast down on someone's head. The psychotics put their arms over their heads and screamed; they saw an avalanche of balls.

I loaned Arthur my Pink Floyd tape and he traded me some New Wave. We liked each other. In his calm voice he said, "I have a car." He didn't mean at the hospital. He meant outside.

"I've got a place to live and a stereo," he said. "We could be together. You know, get married."

At twenty-one, Arthur didn't let his current lockup curb him. He'd been to college, he'd seen the world. He could imagine a regular life with the two of us driving around together. I was flattered he wanted to look me up after we were done with all this. But I wasn't particularly interested. He lived in a different unit so I let him stew.

Fred was a lech. He'd slip his long monkey arms inside his pants in the lounge. A nurse walking by would say, "Fred, stop that. Stop that." Or one of the patients would go up to the nurses' station and say, "Fred's jacking off again."

He pursued me after I'd been moved to the maximum security unit for bad behavior; it was hard to get away from him. When I passed him in the hall he said, "I love you." He had puffy lips and the outside of his mouth was red and irritated. "Hey, really, listen," he said. "You should marry me."

An idea flickered across his face. "If we were married, we could share a room," he said.

"You're not going to get my tape deck, Fred," I said, heading for my room. Everybody wanted something: tape decks, cassettes, radios, sex.

Fred leered at me and unzipped his pants. "You know you want it," he called after me. The nurse raised her head, looked at me, then went back to her charts. It seemed to me she was thinking, Yes, you should marry him. How choosy do you think you can be, young lady? There's not much demand in the marriage market for a girl mental patient who walks tough like a boy.

Fred talked about me to Mike, the guy who dragged around the ceramic snake. This gave Mike his own ideas. When Mike was manic, he was a lot of fun, chatty and smart. We started watching *Wonder Woman* on tv together and soon all the people on the unit who could voice their opinions refused to take medication or go for a bath from three to four p.m. In a hospital, power is determined by talking and walking, or not. So we sat silent and refused to budge from *Wonder Woman*.

The more manic Mike got, the more opinionated he became. He saw himself as a philosopher—on a bad day, he believed he was Jesus, too. "I understand you," he told me. "You need me to take care of you." He leaned toward me. "We could be here forever, together."

We were sitting in the lounge, watching the *Wonder Woman* credits scroll up the screen. I was unmoved by his pleas. "Look, Daphne," he said. At twenty-six, he liked to play the wiser, older man; I was fifteen. "We're stuck in here," he said. "I'm probably the best guy you're going to find, so you should marry me."

He turned to the male attendant who was slumped on the sofa, bored. "Isn't that true?"

"What?" the attendant asked.

"I'm the best guy for Daphne," Mike said.

"Yeah," the attendant said. "That sounds about right."

"Don't bug me," I said.

A skinny guy named Paul skulked around the unit. I didn't even know him. When he got me alone, he said he wanted to do things to my body.

The boy I liked was James. He was a cutie, about twenty-one, a sweet, depressed boy with blond hair so thick it rode on his head like a wave. Sitting around the lounge he wore white-and-blue hospital pajamas because he was on AWOL precautions. The hospital figured that if you ran for it, you couldn't get too far in your Michael Reese pjs.

"I'd definitely get a Mustang convertible," I was saying. "Nothing new. I don't mind rust. Something with a little wear-and-tear on it."

Heather said she'd get a Mercedes or BMW, something that shrieked money. Danny would go for flash, maybe a Jag.

"A Mustang," James said. "That sounds cool." In his pajama bottoms, his erection rose like a tent pole. I looked away and he blushed. He was shy about sex, like me. Later on Danny teased him, called him pup tent.

During the afternoons, Heather and Danny had sex in Danny's room. Another girl had been Danny's girlfriend before Heather showed up and snagged him, the catch of the unit. This change in partners caused a lot of anguish and note-writing among the girls.

For some reason, the staff let Danny do what he wanted. Maybe it was his voice. When he launched into "Precious Blood" they looked up from the nurses' station and smiled. He played to them, tilting his eyes down so everyone could see his long lashes. He owned an elegant black suit he wore for visitors. The nurses let him hang fishnet from the ceiling of his room and looked the other way about the lighter he hid beside his bed. He was suave.

Left behind while Heather and Danny disappeared, James and I decided that sex was something we'd try, too.

A couple of days later, James drifted up the hall and I watched him duck into my room. I was roommate-less for a few weeks. Not only did I have a room to myself, I had my own bathroom. About five minutes later, I got up from the lounge as if the idea had just occurred to me.

James was sitting on the edge of the bathtub. We looked at each other, nervous, but we didn't have a lot of time to futz around. I flipped off my sneakers, toe to heel, slid off my pants. James did the same. His legs were muscular, with blondish hair. He kissed me standing up and I thought about how all the other patients were going to think this was so cool, James and I doing it in my bathroom. The tile floor was a rectangle too small to lie down on and he was a lot taller than I was. I could stand on the edge of the tub, or he could sit on the toilet; we tried to figure it out.

Someone knocked on the door. "We know you're in there."

James said, "Oh, shit."

"Come out or we'll come in after you."

We pulled on our clothes and walked out, la, la, la. After that, they watched us.

I liked James and I was curious, but I never really wanted to have sex with anyone. I couldn't admit that, though. I didn't want to say I was scared.

A letter to Nurse Kay:

. . . At this time (10:40 p.m.) I'm feeling pretty good. I just took my sleeping med., and tonight I won my first spades game. I also got an excellent phone call from my sister, she's doing real good . . . I want to talk to you later about my sister and my mother's boyfriend and also my mother's father. In other words everything that has been happening lately. Well, I really gotta go (school tomorrow). It's 11:00 and I'm feeling really drowsy! But if it's possible, come up and see me tomorrow or the next day (PLEASE)! I would really like it.

p.s. I have been trying throughout this letter not to bring up adoption but I had to say that I'm not going to give up and I wish you would reconsider!

Love you lots and think of you all the time!
Daphne

S I X

SOME DAYS *my mother perked up and came to*

my school. She was the art mom for the class and

showed us pictures by Braque, Van Gogh and

Picasso and I felt proud she knew things other moms

didn't. All the elementary kids rode on a bus to see

the Picasso statue in front of a brick building in our

town. The principal said how lucky we were to live

so close to genuine art even though everyone knew

Picasso didn't even finish the statue himself, he died and someone else finished it. Besides, the statue was an obese woman with huge boobs and out-of-proportion body parts. We stood around but I looked at my sneakers. Body parts embarrassed me.

The other thing that perked up my mother was when she opened the black mailbox and she found her Ms. magazine. She explained that Ms. was what girls and women should be called and I was Ms. Scholinski. She took me out of school to ride the bus to an Equal Rights Amendment rally in Springfield and I swung in the aisle holding onto the black plastic handles. Afterward, my mother and father fought in the car about me missing school and he said he was all for women's rights, but a child needs to go to school. Helen Reddy was on the radio singing "I Am Woman" which my mother turned up when it came on, an annoyance to my father. I sat in the backseat and sang the part about hear me roar which made my father drive the car extra crazy. My mother thought all the time of leaving my father but decided that was immature.

My mother announced that she wasn't going to sit around the house anymore, she was going to get a job and she did. She found another hearing-aid place where she could be the manager. This was so if she needed to, she could bring Jean and me to work with her and no one could argue.

At home we got a babysitter named Margo, a high-school senior with a love of fire. She kept her long hair permed and globbed on the eye makeup. Everything was jeans: jean skirt, jean jacket. When Margo served us macaroni and cheese for dinner she lit the candles on the table and ran her finger through the flame. Jean's face pinched into a serious expression as Margo moved her finger closer and closer. Jean said, "Stop it." I said, "Cool," and ran my finger through the flame, just to try it. The flame was warm but I could take it.

One afternoon Margo piled her school books into the Weber grill in the backyard, squirted lighter fluid and threw in a match. Whoosh, a bonfire. I was in the living room when I saw the orange flames shimmering in the window glass. Outside, I stood on the grass and stared at the fire. I put my fingernail in my mouth for a good chew. The pages of the books crinkled into smoky black ash, then the heat reached the lighter fluid and the whoosh happened again. I didn't think the fire looked cool; it was ten feet from the house. I thought it should be put out.

My parents took the bonfire as a sign of irresponsibility. They fired Margo and hired her younger sister, Gloria.

When Gloria was over Jean and I played house. I was the child and Jean pretended to mash up potatoes for dinner and I said, "No, you're not doing it right, a good mother knows you must mash them up hard," and she'd mash harder and pretend to spoon-feed me. We'd pull blankets over the chairs in the living room and sit under them. Just the two of us, telling stories to each other. We'd be wearing the matching outfits my mother sewed for us—white Snoopys on an emerald-green background.

Gloria wanted to play so we let her and after a while she said, "I have an idea for a game. I'll be the doctor and you be the patients." Pretty soon the game was the same every time. She had to check us out for medical problems so we'd better sit still on our beds with nothing on but a tee shirt. "There, that's good," she'd say in a sugar voice. "Now I want to make sure you aren't sick but you don't want to tell your parents, you don't want them to worry, do you?" I didn't know what to say. Gloria was a teenager with a Levi's jean jacket and she liked Jean and me. No words came out of my mouth. She touched me where I didn't want to be touched and I let her do it so what could I say, anyway? I felt the badness inside me.

One night I walked into our room and Gloria had Jean alone for an exam. She'd never done this, it had always been the three of us together. Jean was mine to protect, but how? I said, "I'm hungry," and stood there until Gloria and Jean got off the bed and we all went into the kitchen to find food. When my mother got home I got up my nerve and told her that I didn't want Gloria in the house anymore. We'd never complained about babysitters before so my mother said okay.

MY FATHER GROCERY SHOPPED without a list, pushed the cart down every aisle into the meats and the canned goods. Walking beside him, I pointed at things I liked. My father stopped and considered, he bought nothing without deliberation. After a while I said, "I have to go to the bathroom," and he said, "You can hold it," and I said, "No I can't," and set out to find the bathroom myself. This was a clean suburban store with a bathroom in the back by the oniony smelling produce. On the door it said: WOMEN. As I left the bathroom, a balding clerk with wet produce stains on his apron gave me a look of raw hatred. He grabbed my hand. He wanted to know where my parents were and I said my father was in the aisles.

We looked down each one until we saw him pausing before the cereal. The clerk hauled me over and said, "We found your son in the women's bathroom."

My father said calmly, "That's not my son," which caused the clerk to go into fits and demand to know who my real parents were. My father explained that I was his daughter. The clerk blushed up to his hairline. "I'm sorry, sir. I thought she was a boy." I looked at the tiles on the floor but no one apologized to me and everything bad I felt inside lumped onto the fact that I did not look right.

I wore Toughskin jeans with double-thick knees so I could wrestle with Jean and the neighborhood boys. My mother cut my hair short so my father wouldn't brush my long-hair snarls with No More Tangles spray that was a bunch of crap. I took off my shirt in the summer when the heat in Illinois smothered me in the yard and I got on my bike and glided down the hill no-handed. The wind on my chest felt like freedom until three boys from my neighborhood saw me and said, Daphne, let me see your titties, which was ridiculous since my chest was as flat as theirs but they held me on the ground. My ride was ruined and I put on a shirt, but not before I punched one of them hard in the stomach and they all backed off.

Still, I got no end of grief. We were in the supermarket again and I went to the bathroom and another clerk saw me come out. Same reaction. After he dragged me down the aisle to my father to say I'd been in the ladies' room, my father took my hand and slapped it.

"Bad boy," he said. "I told you to stop doing that."

I did not know what to think.

MY FATHER had a brown oiled mitt and bought me a smaller one and we threw the ball in the backyard. From the start I could throw and catch and with the sun out and the smell of grass I wanted to play baseball. My mother said, Let's drive over to Little League, and the coach took me on the Padres team. *This girl Kimmy and I were the first girls in the league. Kimmy was a fine-boned fluff-ball with a little scarf around her neck, couldn't throw or hit. Didn't even try. The boys liked her but hated me because I wanted to play for real.*

The Padres were losers. So many kids signed up for Little League that year that there was an overload so they took all the new kids and stuck them on the Padres. When I swung my bat at the plate Mr. Spinelli, the coach, yelled, "You're never going to get a hit that way." I swung clean through the air, three times. He said, "What did I tell you, you're never going to get a hit that way."

His son, Vinny, had a feeble throwing arm for a pitcher. "You're never going to make it into the plate with that kind of throw," Mr. Spinelli said, and we watched the ball fade in the dirt before the plate. Vinny looked at the grass. His father made him keep pitching even though Vinny had to put his elbow in a plastic bucket of ice when we weren't on the field. I felt sorry for Vinny having to get in the car with his father after practice and hear about his pitching faults all the way home. But it was hard to feel too sorry because I could throw farther than Vinny which made Mr. Spinelli hate me, so he banished me to deep right field and last in the batting order.

My mother sat in the green bleachers at every practice. She said Mr. Spinelli was a male chauvinist pig.

During the change-up the boys on the team walked up to me and said, "Why are you trying to be a boy?" Mr. Spinelli could hear them but he never said anything. A boy with curly hair that stuck out on the sides of his baseball cap said, "Tomboy, tomboy," and I said, "Yeah, so what, I'm going to kick your butt."

After every game, my mother said we needed something to lift our spirits so we drove to Baskin-Robbins and I got a mint-chocolate-chip cone. Flecks of chocolate in green ice cream. For my mother, butter-pecan.

In the very last game of the season, I made my first hit. I swung, and the bat connected with the ball. For a second I had to think about what to do next. All this time I'd been concentrating on watching the ball and shifting my weight; I'd never thought about running the bases. The ball skidded on the ground between shortstop and second base and I got moving. I crossed first base, easy. I stood on the bag, all smiles. The next batter up made the third out and my mini–reign of glory was over.

The next year I wanted to play Little League again but my mother said, "Are you sure you want to do this? Let's try girls' softball instead."

The softball came at me so big and slow it gave me time to think of all the different ways I could smash it. The Little League drills paid off and I hit home runs as if they were nothing. When I came up to the plate the other team called time out so the fielders could move back. I played first base, I was the cleanup batter, I was the power hitter. The fielders on our team had nothing to do because the pitcher and I made all the outs at first.

My mother would drive up in the white Dodge Dart with me in the passenger seat and the girls would yell, Daphne's here.

We won games. Now the whole team went to Baskin-Robbins afterward.

MY FATHER TOOK an architecture job in South Carolina which was strange since we lived in Illinois. My mother said it was the last straw, he wasn't trying anymore. After almost a year he came back and started sleeping squashed on the couch. To roll over he had to lift himself up and flip like a cylinder.

This put him in a mood. After my shower one morning I passed through the living room on the way to my bedroom, with just my underpants on, as usual. I was ten years old with a body like a twig. Walking in from the kitchen, my father looked at my half-naked body and fury overtook him. He shouted, Cover yourself, cover yourself, as if my skin were on fire. I dove behind the couch, screaming for my mother, who rushed downstairs to see about the commotion. Get her a towel for God's sake, my father told her. I crouched low with my hands holding on to the top edge of the couch, my bare feet damp on the orangey matted carpet.

After this I couldn't take off my clothes in the locker room for gym class. I faked a note from my father that I had knee pain and couldn't exercise and when the authority of the note ran out I huddled up in a toilet stall and changed into my gym uniform. I didn't want anyone to see me naked.

MY MOTHER *said she had to save herself, she had a plan. Jean and I would stay with our father so we wouldn't have to change schools and leave our friends. She would go to Chicago and get an apartment with a roommate and go to college to study film. We'd been to Chicago before, a long drive, more than an hour. She'd taken us to the Art Institute and the Field Museum where the tyrannosaurus rex skeleton stood in the entranceway. I wasn't afraid of the tyrannosaurus even though my teacher said it was the meanest, most powerful creature. To me, he was probably misunderstood. I thought if I'd met the tyrannosaurus when he was alive we'd be friends; I'd understand that he was a sweety underneath and he'd think the same of me.*

My mother said we could visit her on weekends.

I stood on the concrete doorstep outside the house next to the geranium pots. My mother backed out in the white Dodge with her suitcases and I wanted to go to Chicago with her. I'd leave behind the grocery clerk who hauled me out of the bathroom and the Little League boys who called me tomboy. I'd go to the city and I wouldn't bother my mother, I'd find my own food.

I couldn't even tell her this because she was already gone.

Our gas got cut off for nonpayment. My father said my mother had let the bill go too long, so he cooked on the green two-burner Coleman stove with the flip-up lid on the kitchen counter. He pressure-cooked potatoes even though we hated them. Heated up lima beans, which were worse. "You're not leaving the table until your plate is empty." When my father wasn't looking, we mashed up the limas and stuffed them into the metal rods under the table.

Jean and I boiled up a pot of water and I carried it to the sink since there was no hot water in the faucet. We washed our hair but after we squeezed on the creme rinse the water pot was empty. We stuck our heads under the cold faucet which made our scalps red and numb.

We weren't as clean as our classmates, which bothered my neatly groomed sister. At the park, a kid named Earl said Jean was scuzzy. She was in second grade, I was in sixth, and she was chubby in a cute way. Her chubbiness was part of what people picked on. The other thing was no one was washing her clothes so she wore the same dress and pants alternating days and they gave off a smell.

My father wasn't one to notice. He'd taken me to JCPenney to get my first bra, an occasion that mortified both of us. He was so bashful he kept his eyes on the store carpet and walked up to a woman and mumbled about his daughter needing a bra. I had to nudge him and say, "She's not real, Dad. She's a mannequin." He found a sales clerk who briskly took charge and handed me two white training bras, 28A.

One day Jean and her friends were playing girls against the boys, each side hurling rocks at the other, when Earl lobbed a stone that hit her skull. I was over playing baseball in the open area where the tree seedlings were the bases. She came looking for me, her hand on her head. When she found me she lifted up her hand and blood poured down through her hair onto her yellow YMCA tee shirt. She screamed.

Rage sparked inside me. Jean was like my own child, my baby, and aside from Miss Martin, she was the only one who gave me love. She looked up to me. When I sang lead vocals to Blondie songs into my tape recorder, she'd lie on the rug next to me and sing backup, la, la, la. She couldn't remember the words and I could, which impressed her.

She told me Earl threw the rock. With Jean breathing ragged, sobbing, we walked to her friend Lizzy's house. Lizzy's mother opened the door and I handed Jean over.

Earl was on his bike, riding through the trails, and I was on foot so I cut through people's backyards. By the time he got to his driveway I was standing right there. He dropped his bike on the ground and ran into the house. Without a knock, I followed him in. His mother said, "What are you doing in my house?"

I said, "Your son threw a rock at my sister's head, she's bleeding all over the place and I'm going to kick his ass."

She said, "No, you're not," so I had to go home.

The next day in the hall on the way to recess I punched Earl in the stomach and knocked him down. Nothing happened to me for punching him and I wouldn't *have cared if anything did. My mother was gone and layers were piling on top of me, layers and layers. I knew I wasn't being good and polite and a role model for Jean but my teachers and my father and my mother didn't believe I ever could be anyway, so why should I try? I couldn't see out from the layers on top of me and no one could see in.*

SEVEN

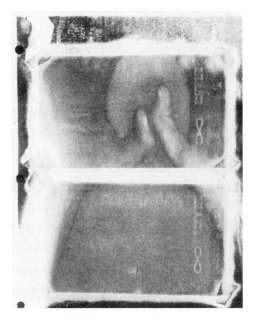

I GOT A ROOMMATE. Francine had a

sagging face with cheeks that drooped like

a dog's. Long before she became my

roommate she'd given up, or else the fight

had been zapped out of her. She was about

fifty, wicked depressed, and wore blue

hospital slippers like foot mittens. They

made a sandpapery sound as she inched

her way across the linoleum in her housecoat.

Twice a week at six-thirty a.m. I'd hear the electroshock cart squeak down the hall and pull up outside our door. A nurse would come in and put her hand on my shoulder and say, "Time to get up," and I'd drag myself out of the room.

After they'd leave, her sleeping face would be slack. One morning when the shock team came—one doctor, two nurses and three attendants—I pretended to be in a deep sleep. It wasn't anything I'd planned. I was tired and wanted to sleep. Then again, the hospital was also my high-school education. I wanted to know what happened when the cart rolled into my room.

The nurse gave up trying to wake me. "She's out," she said. I cracked open my eyelids and watched them dab paste on Francine's temples, where the wires connected. The nurse stuck a gauze gag into Francine's mouth.

"Ready?" the doctor asked. The others nodded.

"Set?" A warning beep sounded and the team braced themselves, six pairs of shoes firm on the floor—all of them white except for the doctor's dressy black ones. A second beep went off, this one a long beep that lasted the duration of the shock. Francine's body shook and all six of them couldn't hold her down. The muscles in her neck stood out, her back arched, drool streamed out her lips.

The shock ended. Then they did it again.

Francine lay absolutely still when they were done. I couldn't wake her up for anything. All day I stayed in our room waiting for her to come back to life. When she did, she couldn't remember what had happened to her, or that the day before her son—her only joy—had visited.

"Was it a good visit?" she asked.

I told her I thought it was.

Later that week, she said she was thirsty. I offered her a drink of water.

She said, "Oh, no, I can't have that. I'm not allowed to drink the night before treatment."

I asked her if she wanted the treatments and she said no, so we made a deal. I would give her a drink and she would go tell the nurse that I had.

The nurse came right in and asked me if I'd given Francine

water, and I said yes. Francine didn't get the treatment the next day. We did it again. The muscles on her face started working; she figured out how to smile.

In the morning, the nurse came into the room and told us we were being separated. I was being moved out. Francine's treatments began again.

In my new bed I dreamed about watching Francine get shocked. The shock kept going, it wouldn't stop. On the unit, when Columbia said, You'd better start acting right, I flashed on Francine, her body moving into positions I'd never imagined, contorting in pain. A new kind of fear blew through me. I knew it could happen to me.

LIFE WAS WORSE downstairs in 2 West. The hallway smelled of unwashed underarms, urine in the pants, vomit. The people looked as if their bodies and minds had been separated so long that all communication had broken down. Their clothes were skewed, their hair wild, their faces twisted up with all the terror that wanted to spill out.

I thought, This is how the outside world sees me: insane.

The parents of my father's girlfriend sent me a card: *Get well soon.* It was considerate of them, but it made me feel worse.

Nobody slept soundly on 2 West. If your own anxiety didn't keep you up, somebody else's would—all that late-night hysteria. 2 West meant plastic cutlery, no shoelaces, and seclusion.

I got sent to 2 West a couple of times, once for being fresh to Columbia.

On 3 East and West, we'd been watching tv, one of the afternoon soaps, when Bob came in and started preaching. He was Jesus and Jesus didn't approve of the soaps.

"Television is evil," he said. He may have been right, but television was all we had. Someone told him to shut up. He said it again: "Television is evil."

Columbia piped up. "It's stupid to argue over tv. Why would anyone argue over tv?" She thought of us as doomed idiots and we tried to live up to her opinion. "You're all so childish," she said.

I called her a bitch. She told me to go to my room and I told her no, and swore at her a couple of times, and she said, "All right, that's it." We knew what that meant: security was coming. Muscular guys from the south side of Chicago who wore white uniforms.

Three, four, five minutes passed before they arrived. Enough time for me, in shorts and a tee shirt, to run into my room and slather baby oil on my arms and legs. Three guards showed up and surrounded me and when they reached for my shiny wrists I slid out of their hands. I ran all over the unit, through the lounge, jumping over the sectional furniture. I ran with a manic fury, the way I ran from my father when I broke out of his room after he hit me with his belt. I laughed, even though I knew what was coming.

I skidded down the hall past Mike, who was walking his ceramic snake, dragging it behind him with a telephone cord. He hugged the wall when he saw me heading his way.

Eventually, the guards caught me; there weren't that many places to run and the guards figured out it would be smarter to grab for my shirt than my oily arms. They pinned me to the floor, twisting my arm so far behind my back it felt as if my shoulder was going to pop out. Then came the quick footsteps of the nurse bearing a syringe full of Thorazine. From the corner of my eye I saw the needle coming at me, which made me thrash. The needle-stick burned my thigh and my muscles melted until I was liquid. The guards picked me up and carried me out, heading down to 2 West.

When I woke up the nurse told me to put on a white cotton hospital gown with three ties in the back and a snap at the top. Upstairs the staff had been egging me on to trade my torn-up jeans for a nice dress, which I refused. I don't know what they would have done if I'd said, "Oh, okay, I'd love to wear a dress." I didn't have a dress. None of the other girls wore dresses either. Nurse Kay would wear a white skirt sometimes, and the head nurse, too—that was as close to a dress as we saw on the unit. It was just a routine we went through. Dr. Browning would say, "Why don't you put on a dress instead of those crummy jeans?" and I'd say, "No."

In 2 West I had no choice. A dress was seclusion garb. They led me into the seclusion room, which was nine square feet of whiteness, except for the yellowed sheets on the mattress on the floor. In my hospital gown, I curled up in a ball in the corner, because that's what I thought a person in seclusion was supposed to do.

My first conversation was with Anne. She put her chubby face up to the tiny chicken-wire glass window in the door and said, "I think I'm going to have to kill you."

I curled up tighter, to make myself small, and lay like that a long time. I thought, This is how I'm going to die, curled up in a white room in a mental hospital.

Every hour during the daytime a nurse came in with a cigarette for me. I sat on the mattress and she sat beside me and supervised me while I smoked so I didn't torch anything. Mostly I couldn't think of a thing to say. Sometimes she'd forget to come, unless an hour just seemed so long that I thought she'd forgotten.

In between times I paced. After I got sick of pacing, I beat the concrete wall. With my hand in a fist, I wound up and punched but the wall didn't shake; the wall was as immovable as everything else in my life. It felt normal to be hurting myself; I was surrounded by head-pounders and suicide-attempters and screamers.

After the first punches I couldn't feel the pain. I wanted to break a bone because they'd have to let me out of seclusion to get it fixed, but I never did. Later, shades of purple and blues and blacks, beautiful colors, surfaced from my wrist to my elbow. I thought of Margaret, shitting in her wheelchair upstairs. We all have to find a way to say no.

Because I wouldn't use the bedpan, an attendant escorted me to the bathroom. Mostly the attendants were women, but sometimes it would be a man. Whoever it was would stand in the opening of the bathroom door and sneak looks at me while I sat on the toilet. There'd be a long silence, both of us waiting for something to happen. I'm a private person. The pressure slowed down the whole business. When I had to go to the bathroom with a male escort during my period—I can't even talk about it.

I learned to hold my pee for a long time. I got a bunch of urinary tract infections.

After I was in seclusion for a while, a nurse with a key ring on her belt unlocked the seclusion door and handed me a paperback. I'd been begging for *The Outsiders;* I'd heard about this book—a teenage gang from the wrong side of the tracks. I lay on my mattress and read. This was the first book I read front-to-back, all the way through.

Eventually the nurses let me out. It was hard to know exactly how much time had passed. An attendant led me into a room on 2 West.

Whenever Anne was in the hall, I hid. I didn't forget what she'd said.

None of Anne's eight personalities wanted to see her family, the Cornings. A couple of times a day Anne ran through the unit yelling, "Are the Cornings coming? Are the Cornings coming?"

The attendant ran around after her, telling all of us to calm Anne down and say, No, the Cornings weren't coming.

Everyone was louder in 2 West. My room was next to a woman who yelled, "I want to die. Let me die." It got so no one paid attention to her. Her screaming bugged me but I admired her. At least she was out there with her pain; she wasn't ashamed of it.

This woman hadn't taken a bite of food in two years. Three times a day, mush dribbled into her through tubes in her nose and throat. The attendant said, "Mmm, doesn't that taste good?"

At night she yelled: "Let me die, let me die." I paced in my room with my hands over my ears and shouted, "Let her die."

Farther down the hall, Anne was agitated. "Are the Cornings coming?" she asked. She slept in two-point restraints, one arm, one leg, diagonally tied down. "Are the Cornings coming?" Even in restraints she was strong. She was a large woman. She bounced her bed out of her room and into the hall, thump, screech, thump. Then came the soft-soled sound of the night attendant arriving to push her back into her room.

I grew curious.

One day in the lounge Anne asked me if the Cornings were coming.

"Yeah," I said. "I think I heard them talking about it."

She screamed, reaching for anything she could find: paper cups of water and juice, chairs, cushions. She threw things until the nurse came with Thorazine. I felt horrible. As patients, we tried to stick together. But afterward Anne and I became buddies. She didn't scare me. I'd probably end up like her if I stayed here as long as she had—eight years. The good part was she didn't know she'd been here that long.

Christmas on 2 West was worse than anything. A tree stood in the lounge, ultra fake, with green branches that were bristly but limp, like a soft sculpture. The staff removed the metal supports for the branches so we couldn't use them as weapons to kill ourselves or them. Bulbs and lights were forbidden, no glass, nothing sharp. We had popcorn but we couldn't make chains since we couldn't have a needle. With tape, we stuck the popcorn to the branches. It looked funny.

You could kind of see snow out the security screens on the windows. The nurses said, "Merry Christmas."

My father and his girlfriend sent me a package. Preppy blouses and polo shirts like Heather's, just what I'd asked for, but I was in a bad mood, I hated the clothes, I hated that I couldn't wear what I wanted and be left alone about it so I tore the collars off. Rip, rip. I wore the shirts that way.

After a while, I was sent back up to 3 East and West and when I heard the screamers below, I knew just who they were.

As soon as I got upstairs I ran to Nurse Kay and put my arms around her for a hug and her body stiffened; it was like hugging a board. She smiled and listened to me tell her everything that was going on and I told myself, She's having a hard day, she's tired, it can't be me, it can't be something I've done, she'll adopt me for sure, I'll win her back.

But I couldn't. I don't know what had happened. I'd see her around and say, "Hey, Kay," but when I talked to her she wouldn't look me in the eye. It was as if her mind were somewhere else. I didn't dare mention it because I knew she'd say, "Of course I'm listening," and write in my chart *trust issues.*

A NEW PATIENT CAME onto the unit and we all stared. Tall, slender, trace of an afternoon shadow, a man in a brown wig and an old-lady flowered dress. Sandra, older than sixty. Deaf and couldn't speak. Carried a brown purse around with her. The nurses said she was confused and gave her a private room, since they didn't want to put anyone with her. The electroshock cart stopped at her room, but after it left Sandra didn't look changed. I thought she was tough for that, not to change.

At dinner she sat at the table with the rest of us and it was as if she wasn't there. I studied her. One of the attendants whispered— as if she could hear. "Faggot," he called her, and I told him to shut up.

Putting her meal tray back into the metal cart, Sandra slipped and fell and her dress flew up. We saw she was a man, even though we already knew. We saw it. Her wig slid off her head, lay on the floor next to her bald head. I sat in my seat, frozen, scared. A thin line connected Sandra and me, I didn't know how or why, but I felt it.

Whenever I saw her on the unit, I paid attention. I tried to figure out why I felt sad looking at her. We both weren't appropriate-looking; I knew that much. I couldn't swing my butt like a girl. Sandra was better at it than I was; it seemed to come naturally to her. I didn't look super feminine, even with my hair hanging to my collar; *unkempt*, the attendant called my hairstyle. I was starting to get that mental-patient look.

2/22/82 NOON FELLOW'S NOTE
    Very anxious to re-establish closeness of relation-
ship in spite of need to verbalize scatalogical concerns
& curiosity about sexual issues. She is getting more &
more curious/anxious about these issues as she approaches
having a single room, which appears to be a source of
overstimulation. Issues that are surfacing may not be the
most pleasant for us but absolutely necessary for her development. Our response will provide her with a model of
how reasonable, healthy people handle these subjects
with their children and will fill in an area of mental

structure which she lacks—is deficient in—due to a deficiency in her natural parents.

—, M.D.

"Your behavior is deteriorating," the head nurse said. I didn't care. I felt like being bad. When I was bad, I knew who I was. I understood how I was being seen: the bad girl. It beat being seen as the insane girl.

I got in trouble when the housekeeper found a marijuana pipe in my room; it wasn't mine, I didn't like marijuana, I was hiding the pipe for Danny, but of course I couldn't say that.

I pounded the wall in my room, bam, bam; the throbbing comforted me. On my dinky cassette player I blasted Pink Floyd or AC/DC. Angry, violent songs. I thought of the music as an S.O.S. from me to the world. The reply I got was a nurse telling me to turn that racket down.

When my wrist swelled from the wall-pounding, I had to sit in the lounge with an ice pack.

My restrictions piled up, one on top of the other, just like when my father grounded me: Restricted for not being in bed at 11 p.m., restricted for talking back to staff, restricted for throwing around my ice pack in the hall with another patient.

Escape was something we all talked about. It was a sign of sanity; it was a statement, *I am not one of these people, I am not a mental patient.*

On 3 East and West, we had phones in our room that connected us to the hospital switchboard. Sometimes I had permission to call my mother, my father and Jean. Sometimes I was shut off. I picked up the phone and the operator connected me to a cab company. "Michael Reese Hospital," I said. "Singer Pavillion."

I was on my way to adjunctive therapy in the basement to paint a King Tut mask. I'd been kicked out of art therapy for painting a ceramic dog plaid, tan with thin lines, blue and red. The art teacher said, That doesn't look like a dog. She sent me upstairs, I was restricted from art for two days for painting a plaid dog, now I was back as long as I promised to paint in an acceptable manner.

Art therapy was one of the few occasions that allowed me to go off the unit, but an attendant had to ride with me in the elevator. When she looked away I discreetly pressed the L button, for lobby. The door opened, she looked puzzled and I darted out.

The yellow cab was there, motor running. I jumped in, the driver pulled away from the curb, the attendant ran after us yelling, "Stop! Stop!" We drove. The driver looked in his rearview mirror. "Stop! Stop!" followed us down the block.

He said, "I'm sorry, I'm going to have to let you out."

I didn't know where I was going to go, anyway. And I didn't have any money, either.

I stopped writing to Nurse Kay. She was never going to adopt me—I couldn't even paint a ceramic dog the right way.

3/10/82 9 A.M. FELLOW'S NOTE

Informed about decision to discharge reached due to unworkable situation with parents, their lack of cooperation, and continuing non-compliance by Daphne with hospital rules and staff limits which has resulted in continuous struggling to establish a working alliance rather than actual treatment. It is felt that since this has not occurred over six months of hospitalization it will not occur. She became depressed when hearing the decision and will need to be evaluated for suicidal risk during the next few days. About 30 days has been given to work on separation from hospital to discharge.

——, M.D.

The hospital was kicking me out. Who gets kicked out of a mental hospital? Failing in school was one thing—truancy, mouthing off, not attending class: all good reasons for being kicked out. But even Anne got to stay in a mental hospital, screaming and throwing fits and switching personalities without warning. I thought I must be so psycho I didn't even know it.

It was March; I'd been at Michael Reese for six months. Through the lounge window you could see the spidery limbs of the tree outside.

Dr. Browning told me that in order for me to remain at Michael Reese, my parents had to be involved and my parents had refused.

The whole staff knew, of course. My art therapist said my parents had a lack of commitment to caring for me. *A lack of commitment to caring for me:* those were her words. I watched her mouth move and what I heard was *worthless trash.*

EIGHT

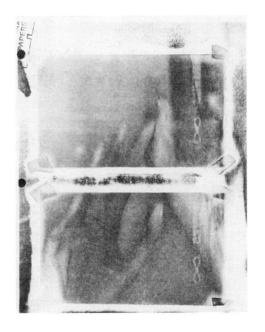

AFTER MY MOTHER *moved out, my father went grocery shopping by himself. He'd drop the bundles on the counter and say, This has to last for two weeks. Inside the bags were frozen lima beans, frozen corn, Cheerios, Total, milk, mustard, mayonnaise, pork chops and bread. By the end, Jean and I were eating mayo and mustard sandwiches. For dessert, squished Wonder bread with sugar on it.*

If there was dog food, we knew Pudgy, our dachshund, was going to be around for a while. My father said, If Pudgy pees on the floor one more time, I'm going to get rid of him. After school, Jean ran into the house and searched the kitchen floor for puddles on the fake-brick linoleum. If she found one she wiped it up with paper towels and pushed the evidence deep into the trash. With Pudgy in her arms she walked around the house, shushing him. Once when my father's threats got serious Jean gathered up Pudgy, a jar of peanut butter and an apple. She barricaded herself in her room with her dresser against the door. Her plan was to stay in there forever. After a while my father stood outside her door and said, "You've got to come out. Listen to me, Jean. You've got to come out." She wouldn't open the door until he said Pudgy could stay.

Sometimes my father let Pudgy be a dog in the world. He'd lift him up and put him in the kitchen sink for a bath. Pudgy wet was skinny and shaking and we thought he looked funny, his toenails scrambling on the stainless steel; it was mean to laugh at the dog when he was scared but it was fun to be laughing together, the three of us. Jean and I would suds up Pudgy and my father would rinse him off and we'd be like a regular family, doing a project.

When my father had a date at night we'd all drive over in the brown Cutlass. "I won't be long," he'd say, and disappear up the sidewalk into a brick apartment building. As soon as he was gone I slid over into the backseat so Jean and I could play war. My seat belt was my gun and the stoplight at the end of the block was our signal. When it turned green, I could fire. Red meant I had to stop. Yellow, maybe, maybe not. When I got wounded, Jean bandaged my arm because she was a nurse.

I wore my puffy blue bubble jacket, with feathers in it. Jean's jacket was pink. We got cold sitting there. Looking at all the windows in the building we tried to figure out which apartment my father was in. If we knew that, we'd know which doorbell to ring. We waited, playing tick-tack-toe on the steamed-up car windows. Then I shouted, Cuddle, cuddle, cuddle, and Jean and I scooched up next to each other and hugged to stay warm. Sometimes we'd fall asleep. When my father came out, he'd drive us home and carry us into the house.

Weekends when we weren't going to my mother's, my father said we had a lot of housework to do and he meant it and it was time for us to pull our weight. Then he sat down on the couch and turned on the tv, Star Trek, Charlie's Angels, Hart to Hart, and smoked cigarettes. Watching tv was the only time I saw him pay attention and look straight at something as if it were extremely fascinating. He'd sit through the commercials and the late-night shows until he fell asleep, folded down on the cushions. Jean would wake me up in the morning and we'd turn the channel to find a show he liked, Cisco Kid, Bonanza, and when he woke up on the couch he started watching again. Pretty soon the afternoon movie would come on and if it was James Bond my father would sit up, all excited. I'd sit beside him, all revved up, too, because he was. My father loved Bond's sports car with the ejection seat, his women with their cleavage falling out of their dresses. We watched every James Bond movie. Afterward I looked at my ballpoint pen and imagined it was a Bond pen with poison darts shooting out of it, pffth, pffth.

We'd order out for pizza and then we'd do it all over again on Sunday. Monday came and we hadn't done a lick of cleaning. The house smelled like pizza grease and cigarette butts and my father said he wasn't going to clean up this goddamn mess so we put the pizza boxes with the other ones on the counter in the kitchen, being careful to walk around Pudgy's pee stains in our bare feet.

I broke a house rule. "You know that thermostat does not go above seventy." He ordered me into his bedroom and I walked down the hall and he turned the lock in the door. From the rack in his closet he lifted off a brown belt and told me to kneel on the floor and lean facedown on the bed. His voice was like a stranger giving orders. This wouldn't have happened if my mother were here, this wouldn't have happened. He folded the belt in two in his hands and snapped it. Tears came to my eyes. He snapped the belt again. He said he'd give me something to cry about and whipped my butt, my legs, my back. Crying made the belt fly harder, so I gave that up and concentrated on how to get away. "I have to pee," I said, and he said, "Hold it," and I said, "I can't, I'm going to pee on your bed." He said, "Okay, you can go to the bathroom as long as you come right back in here." He wasn't a fool but he talked like one sometimes.

Jean sat on the stairs outside the room. Sat there with her head down. She never got hit because she was well mannered, a model for me, my father would say. We had a system. When I came out of the room to go to the bathroom she put my jacket by the door. I rushed out of the bathroom, grabbed my jacket and took off.

When we went to visit our mother, my father dropped us at the train for Chicago and Jean and I climbed to the upper level where the cool people sat with their feet on the railing, looking down at the passengers on the lower level. For a while it seemed the conductor had forgotten about us and we'd get to keep the money but then he came through and stopped underneath us, so we could see his navy blue cap with its hard bill. We handed down our money and he punched two tickets and stuck them in the band of metal at our feet.

When we got to Union Station my mother was out front in the white Dodge looking the same but different. Taxis honked; a man selling hot dogs jabbered away in Spanish. We breathed different air but even with the crowds there was more room in Chicago.

We didn't tell my mother about home. Jean and I didn't tell the first time the heat got cut off. After my father paid the bill and the heat was back on it had some-how been decided between us that we wouldn't talk about home. We didn't want my father to look bad.

My mother lived in a brick apartment building on Farwell Street with a room-mate named David. It was a solid, spacious place, with built-in cabinets and book-cases. My mother and David passed a joint between them at the kitchen table in between sips of vodka while I leaned on my elbows and watched. I asked, "What does vodka taste like?" David said, "It's really strong." I wanted to try some and he said, "It burns, you can't handle it." I said, "I can, too." David poured the vodka into a jigger. My first drink. "Are you sure?" my mother asked. I could see straight through to the little lines on the side of the shot glass. I drank and didn't let my face show how the liquor was like a flaming arrow going down. "That was good," I said. My mother and David looked at each other. I wanted another but my mother said, "No."

After a while I had two lives, city and suburb, and I tried to remember how to act where. In Roselle, I roamed the mall with my friends and everyone watched when the first black family moved in down the street. I played catch with the boy *in the family and when I popped up a high one it broke a window on their house. He told his parents he didn't know anything about the baseball rolling around on the bedroom floor; I appreciated this.*

Anytime a bike was missing, a lot of the white neighbors thought they knew just who to blame.

I never stole a bike but I stole a lot of things—candy, money, small items no one would notice were gone. I don't know why I did it. I didn't let myself think about it. My hands grabbed. I'd go into the 7-Eleven with an empty bag and leave with it full. I just wanted this box of Entenmann's chocolate chip cookies and a carton of Marlboros and a package of Ho-Hos. My school bus stopped in front of the 7-Eleven so I ran in and stuck a whole carton of Bubble Yum down my shirt. On the bus, I handed out Bubble Yum to everyone.

I walked into the new houses in our development. Just walked in. My friend Jeff and I had gone inside when the houses were frames and sheetrock so I knew where all the rooms were. I tried the sliding glass door in back and most times it slid open. Stuck my head in and listened. The stove all shiny and no dog pee on the linoleum floor. In the parents' room, I reached into a jar on the floor next to the bureau where the dad kept his change. I didn't take all the coins, just some. I slipped out the back and went directly to the 7-Eleven and bought soda and gum and looked around for someone to give them to.

I was having trouble with friends. The boys who teased me about not wearing a shirt in the summer came after me, called out "tomboy, tomboy" and knocked my books out of my arms, so other kids stayed away from me. I figured cigarettes and cookies would help me out and they did. I found a friend named Mark and took him to McDonald's. I told him I'd buy whatever he wanted—Big Mac, fries, the works—which he enjoyed.

My father kept his change in a white athletic sock. I dipped into that. Took money from my mother's wallet. Took and took. I wanted the money so I took it.

In my bed at night with Jean breathing next to me and Charcoal the cat purring between my feet I felt the badness like a hand pressing on my face. Everything I couldn't think about during the day drifted back. I saw the sliding glass door opening and me walking through the quiet house, a thief, and the mean faces of the boys on Little League who hated me and yelled, tomboy, tomboy, and my father's glinty eye as he raised the belt in the air. I didn't want to be hated, I didn't want to be a thief, it was just happening. It seemed as if there was nothing I could do to make things right; it wasn't really me doing those things. After a long while, I slipped into sleep.

IN CHICAGO, *my mother, Jean and I were noticeably white, and everyone watched us. I had to walk extra tough in Chicago and regular tough in Roselle.*

Summers I was in the city. No more Schaumburg softball team and Baskin-Robbins and the fat ball coming at my bat. My father forgot to sign me up and anyway, I wanted to be with my mother. Next to my mother's building was a concrete lot. I watched some boys play stickball and they let me play. They said they were in a gang called the Disciples but that didn't scare me because they seemed like regular boys.

Playing stickball, I made two friends, Joey and Luis. Joey ran away from home after his parents split up so he lived wherever he could. His father was in Texas, his mother in California, and he said he could take care of himself. He had a scary look in his eyes, as if he'd do anything.

Luis spoke Spanish and had big curly hair like an Afro and was very protective of his sister when we ran into her on the street. "You'd better get home," he'd tell her. He was the sweet one, who waited a moment before starting to fight, trying to figure out some other way.

Joey and Luis kept twenty-two-caliber pistols tucked in the back of their pants. "If anyone messes with me, I'm going to blow them away," Joey said. "Yeah," Luis said. It was all talk. I never saw them use the guns. They had knives which I never saw them use, either. We sat in the alley and practiced tricks with the knives. I got a butterfly knife which I kept in my sock. Luis said he knew someone who had known Al Capone, no lie. Luis said he was connected to the Mafia, if we ever needed help.

I said I had a bionic arm. Truth. When they weren't looking I'd push in the sides of a Sunkist can to weaken it, then pop the sides out again. While they watched I crushed the can with one hand because of my bionic strength.

Joey flipped his knife in the air, caught it by the handle and said he didn't care if he ever saw his parents again.

"My real father died in Vietnam," I said. "I'm being raised by his best friend who saw my father die. He hits me because I have my father's eyes and he can't stand looking at them because of what they remind him of."

Joey asked did I want to join the Disciples? An honor not offered to many girls. I said, Yeah. A girl Disciple, Vanessa, gave me the first initiation test across from McDonald's. Her nails were sharp and painted red. She scratched down my arm as hard as she could. Blood bubbled up in four lines on my skin. Her pinkie hadn't made a dent.

The second part was to fight to prove I could protect my Disciple brothers in a scene of battle. Joey and Luis circled me on the concrete lot and I didn't know where to look but I was focused just like the way I felt lying on my father's bed with the belt in his hand and me scheming a way out.

The first punch to my stomach made me double over but I stood up and swung back.

Like a cagey animal, I managed to land a blow on Joey's hard stomach. Snot ran out of Joey's nose, he panted and kicked me in the back. I kept my dukes up the way I'd seen in the movies and blocked a couple of punches and no fist got near my head, which made me proud. I landed a punch on Luis's shoulder and he was dead serious looking at me, trying to figure out how to come back at me, but I had him blocked and he decided I'd passed and Joey agreed. They shook my hand and gave me hard hugs which I didn't expect from boys like that.

The Latin Kings and Queens controlled the blocks north of ours and when we saw them on the street we glared and puffed up. If one came near we got ready for a fight but mostly we kept walking. We had our colors. The Disciples were black and blue, the Latin Kings were black and gold, the Royals were blue and red. Outside school, two guys pushed each other, a Disciple and a Latin King. I waited for a Latin King to push me, and when he did, I pushed him, until everyone started backing away down the street, swearing at each other, Hey, fuck you. No, fuck you.

I told Joey and Luis I'd pulled a knife on a guy, but I never had. I had a reputation for being tough, but if it came down to it I was pretty soft. Nobody knew it.

When we were together, Joey and Luis and I would walk into a corner store and start filling our pockets. We took cans of Dinty Moore stew. I think sometimes the cashier saw us but was afraid. Once we took a whole loaf of bread and cans of Dinty Moore and went to my mother's apartment, heated up the stew and ate.

Other times we begged for money under the 'L' tracks so we could buy Mad Dog Twenty-Twenty. In the alley we swigged from the bottle, walked back to the 'L' kind of weaving, stuck our hands out for money. It was a miracle anyone coming off the train gave to us. We pleaded hunger. If someone offered me an orange, I knew to take it, so they wouldn't think I was after liquor. As soon as we had the money we went to the store close to the 'L' tracks where the young guy at the counter didn't care how old we were. He pushed the bottle toward us as soon as we pushed the money toward him.

Luis got in a fight and afterward a cop walked near us. Luis handed me his gun to hold for a few minutes. I stuck it in the back of my pants, the way he did.

I found out I could sell radios at a guy's apartment in Chicago so I took two radios from houses in Roselle and traded them for a wicked boom box that I turned up loud in the park.

One day I was spray-painting scribbles on a garage door on my mother's block and a big man with a red mountain-man beard emerged and said, "What do you think you're doing?"

I said, "Nothing," and put the spray can in a plastic bag. I kept my head down, waiting for the man to yell at me.

He asked, "Do you need some work?"

I said I did.

"Aren't you supposed to be in school?"

I said I didn't like school. I hoped he thought I looked older than thirteen. He looked to be in his thirties, tired around the eyes. His name was Frank. He said he needed someone to help around the house so I started washing his windows and *straightening up.* He had a brown shag rug in the living room and four or five guns mounted on the walls, which I dusted. He said he was a hit man, which I thought was cool, but scary. Thrown on a pile of clothes in his bedroom was a handgun in an ankle holster. He showed me the other gun he wore strapped under his arm and I knew I didn't want to make him mad.

After I cleaned he paid me and told me I was a good kid and the apartment looked clean enough for Christmas. A good kid. He said I was a good kid.

He said, "Do you want some smoke?" and I said, "Yeah," even though I didn't like marijuana. I sucked in my breath and pretended to inhale, to be polite. Here I was a little baby gangster and he was taking me under his wing.

He said, "Are you hungry?" We went out to a home-cooking Polish restaurant where he knew everyone. When the waitress smiled and said, "Hi, Frank," I felt a flush of importance go through me, to be in the company of a man everybody knew. He paid the tab with cash.

Once while I was cleaning he said he was tired, he'd just knocked someone off. Dipped him in cement and thrown him into the Chicago River. I kept my face expressionless. If I did anything wrong, he'd know how to dispose of me.

At first he rubbed my back and I didn't like it but kept quiet because he said I was a good kid. More and more, after I cleaned he asked me to touch him places with my hands and mouth. I split from my body. Just split. It wasn't me doing those things, it wasn't my tongue down his pants.

Two years of this. Frank. He took me out for dinner and gave me money and Ziploc baggies of green marijuana which I gave to my friends. I'd run into him on the street and he'd say, "Why don't you come over later, we can go out to eat?" I knew what he meant but I was hungry. So I went and every time I walked through the door he smiled and said, "Hey, Daphne," as if he were really glad to see me. This made me feel good. I didn't know enough to hate him.

One weekend morning at my mother's, she and I argued, I can't remember what the fight was about. She pushed me and I fell to the floor. She'd never pushed me before. She wasn't like my father, she'd never hit me. But I didn't know she wouldn't hit me someday, who can tell? It seemed to me people walked around with a violent streak inside and if you said the wrong thing the violence ripped out.

To help me up from the floor my mother held out her hand and I thought she was going to hit me so I raised my arm to block her. I struck her face. Never meant to. She ran to her room and turned the lock, click. Talking through the wooden door I told her I wasn't going to hit her, truly I wasn't, but she said, "Go away, I hate you," which were words she'd never said before.

I pleaded some more but she answered me with silence so I left the house. I didn't have a plan in mind but once I was outside I remembered our neighbors, two men with drugs, so I crossed the alley and climbed the back stairs to their apartment. When they saw me they said, Don't be upset, take something to calm yourself. I swallowed a couple of pills, pink, white. All I could think was my mother hates me, my father says I'm out of control, I hit my mother in the face although I didn't mean to. Sitting on a sagging sofa the two men passed a joint, pursing their lips like old ladies. I took a hit, sucked the smoke into my bones, wished for the smoke to carry me away. It did.

By this time the sun was sliding down and I sat on their back steps numb and cold like a rock. I wanted to go home but I couldn't lift my legs. Misty rain made the alley pavement shiny. With concentration I stretched out one leg, then the other, and balanced myself on the ground. When I looked down to see my feet I realized I was blind, my feet were shadowy, but I had to walk anyway.

From the mist a shape came at me and said my name. It was my friend Juan, a chunky, polite guy, and he asked if I was all right. I said, "Sure," and fell backward. When my head smacked the asphalt my teeth chattered. From inside my skull came tiny noises, like wires crackling.

My friend carried me home and my mother's roommate called an ambulance because my mother had gone out. When we got to the hospital, the nurse said I could not be treated without parental permission, there were liabilities to be considered and where were your parents, anyway? She grew irritated dialing my father and then my mother and no one picking up the phone at either place. Finally, my father returned home from wherever he'd been. He said, couldn't he give his okay over the phone? The nurse said no, it was policy, he had to drive in and sign the papers, which put him in a foul mood.

NINE

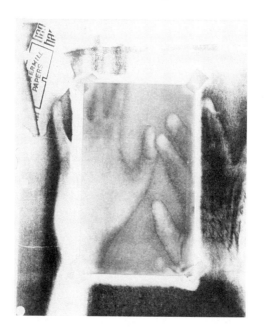

3-11-82 (4-12:30 a.m.)
Daphne remains sad, withdrawn & isolated
in room w. radio on. Anxious, seen
crying at one time. Had been nervous
shown by trembling of extremities,
hyperventilation and cold, clammy hands.
Pt was staring blankly when I came
inside her room. . . . Dr. Browning
called. Medication ordered.

—, P.A.

3-12-82 (10:45 a.m.) Daphne appeared <u>very</u> depressed
in class this morning. She tried to work & said she
could not concentrate. When she was out of the room
briefly the other two students expressed their deep concern for her. She is not communicating with any of her
peers which is not at all her usual behavior. Her depression and despair are such that I feel there may well
be suicidal ideation at this time.

——, M.A.

My mother told me later that the hospital was wrong to say
that they were throwing me out because she wasn't coming to sessions. She said she'd been talking once a week with a counselor at the
hospital; my father also attended, separately, although he'd missed
sessions because they were during the day. Even if he left work early,
the highways were slick with ice and he couldn't always get there on
time. The hospital wouldn't schedule any appointments after 5 p.m.

But I didn't know this then. I still don't know where the truth
rests.

According to my mother, Dr. Browning told my parents that I
was way out of control, disruptive to the unit, and the hospital
couldn't help me. I was too far gone.

My parents believed this.

Now my mother thinks it was a question of insurance. Insurance
money is the subtext of hospitalizations; it can make diagnoses
come and go. Having a fat insurance policy can keep patients around
for months, for observation. After my first six months at Michael
Reese, my father's insurance company would have asked the doctors
to justify keeping me. My mother thinks the doctors at Michael
Reese didn't want to have their treatment plan scrutinized—particularly the Gender Identity Disorder part. I'm not so sure. I know
how sneaky psychiatrists can be, how they can use words to make a
person into whatever they want. Scrutiny does not intimidate them;
they can finesse anything.

Also, the insurance company paid for me to go somewhere else,
where my refusal to wear a dress was of interest to the doctors, so

it couldn't have been just about the diagnosis. I still don't real, know why they transferred me.

One night the nurse found me on my bed, staring, and brought me into the lounge so she could keep an eye on me. I paced for a while, then lay on the couch. The nurse brought out my blanket and pillow so I could sleep in the lounge. Wrapped up in the blanket was my stuffed bunny rabbit. I don't remember who gave me the bunny, but I liked to sleep with it in my arms. It was brown and floppy. I loved the bunny, but not in the lounge. Not when other people could see it.

I tucked the bunny under my arm and carried it back to my room.

On the lounge sofa, I couldn't sleep. The nurse put on soft music from the all-night channel on tv. Easy listening. I closed my eyes.

THE IDEA OF killing myself came into my head. I went back and forth about it. I couldn't figure out a reason to live. Nurse Kay had been my reason, and before her, Jean, and Miss Martin from third grade. Kay was distant, Miss Martin was long gone and I thought Jean had forgotten about me. She couldn't visit me on the unit because she was too young. Anyway, how could I help her when I was going to be locked up for the rest of my life?

In family therapy, my father had said I had to get my act together. How? No matter what I did, my act was not together.

I told Heather I was going to kill myself, which in the realm of suicide attempts indicates a certain desire to fail. But if I was always going to be locked up in some hospital, I might as well kill myself and get it over with.

"You'll get out," Heather said, but I didn't believe her.

I looked around in art therapy for something poisonous I could swallow but the teacher was like a hawk. Slicing my wrist was tricky, since the staff did a silverware count after every meal. If one piece was missing they put the unit through hell: body search, in which we had to strip to our underwear, and room search, in which the dresser drawers were emptied onto the floor. Even if they found the missing knife or fork or spoon in the first room they searched, they still searched every person and every room. This was to make the rest of us furious at the person who stole; the collective rage was supposed to keep someone else from stealing silverware.

Often no silverware was missing—the staff had miscounted, but they never said they were sorry.

One day in my bathroom I noticed the writing on the back of my bottle of Sea Breeze facial astringent. It said, If swallowed, call poison control. I thought, Yes. I snuck the bottle out of the bathroom and hid it in my drawer.

I was waiting for the right moment, the right reason to give up. When it came it was just a little reason, but enough. I was talking to my father on the phone. He said his car had been stolen. From his tone of voice, I felt as if he wanted me to do something about his stolen car. I've always been this way, thinking I should be able to fix everyone else's problems. I couldn't help him, though. I was locked up in a mental hospital which was kicking me out because my doctor said my father and mother didn't care enough about me to show up for appointments.

"What am I supposed to do about your car?" I asked. We got into a fight and I thought, That's it. I'm doing it. I thought I'd be doing him a favor. I imagined that when the hospital called my parents and told them I'd killed myself they'd think, It figures. That's just what Daphne would do—she's so fucked up.

I had the bottle of Sea Breeze on my bureau. Lighter fluid was a last-minute inspiration. I don't know how I got my hands on the bottle; we were allowed to refill our Zippos only while a nurse watched. There was always a lot of refilling going on to keep the smokers happy so maybe I grabbed the bottle when no one was looking.

Standing up, I took a chug of lighter fluid, then a chug of Sea Breeze. Lighter fluid is oily; Sea Breeze is tart and harder to swallow. It didn't go down easily but I'd had some practice swallowing. One of our pastimes on the unit was to drink mouthwash for the alcohol content: to us, peppermint mouthwash was peppermint schnapps; cinnamon was cinnamon schnapps. Cinnamon was our favorite.

I finished off both bottles, then stretched out on my bed, wondering if I'd fall into the long sleep of the dead. This seemed a better way to go than the suicide attempt of another girl on the unit; she'd tried to crush her skull. She'd put her head between the metal bars of her hospital bed and pushed the button that made the top of the mattress tilt up. She didn't succeed, either.

Heather found me in my room. She smelled the lighter fluid and ran for the nurse. Security guys rolled me away on a stretcher to 2 West, but I don't remember this. My memory goes back to lying on the bed and then stops. It happened fast. I found out later that the doctors wouldn't pump my stomach. Poison control said no, wait it out.

When I woke up, I was on a mattress on the floor in seclusion, wearing a blue-and-white Michael Reese hospital gown. Why the hospital would lock me in a room by myself when I felt so sad I wanted to die, I don't know.

Pretty soon a psychiatrist came in to talk to me. She was a sub for my regular doctor, who was on vacation. I liked her—the first female doctor I'd seen. "Suicide is a selfish act," she said. "Do you know that?"

I tried to look repentant.

"An important part of growing up is taking responsibility for your actions," she said. "Do you realize this?"

She saw the incomprehension on my face. "I'm afraid you're not going to be getting out of seclusion until you can take responsibility for your actions," she said.

She left me alone so I could mull over these ideas.

All I could think was, How can I get out of here?

The light bulb glared in the seclusion room. I couldn't get away from it, even with my eyes closed.

The next time I saw her, or the time after that, I said, "I'm sorry." The words were not true, but they had the conviction of desperation. "I understand I have to take responsibility for my actions," I said. "And that I should think of my parents."

After the nurses led me out of seclusion and into a room on the unit, they tied my wrists and ankles to the bed with leather straps: four-point restraint. They said this was so I wouldn't hurt myself.

Every hour the nurse opened the door for checks. At night, the nurse shined a flashlight in my face to make sure I was still there.

Lying in a room by yourself, tied to a bed, makes the time drag. The nurse said, "Let's roll you into the lounge to socialize."

I said, "I'll go if you let me out of restraints."

"Nope, can't do that."

"I want to go out and be normal," I said, and she said, "It's in restraints or not at all." I still didn't want to go but she wheeled me out anyway.

Mike was in the lounge watching tv. "Well, look who we have here," he said. "Can I sit on your bed?"

"Get off my bed," I said.

Fred winked at me. "Let me lie down, I'm tired," he said.

I started working on my right wrist restraint. It was a wide leather bracelet, tied tight to the bed frame. Collapsing my hand I could almost squeeze out of it. I worked and worked on it. My hand came free. "Hey!" I said, holding up my hand.

A male attendant jumped up. "That's it for you, young lady. No more privileges." He tied my wrist again and rolled me out of the lounge into my room. I was glad.

"Bye-bye," Mike said.

Sometime in the night while I slept, Fred crept up to my bed and ran his damp hands over my body. I flinched in my restraints, saw his pug face. He lifted his hands and fled. I heard his heavy walk, then the door sighing closed behind him. In the morning, it never occurred to me to tell the nurses. I thought they'd blame me, twist everything around, make me out to be a flirt in my hospital gown.

We all have to find a way to say no. When Fred entered my room, I wish I'd been able to shout, "No contact! No contact!" I wish I'd known enough to say, I do not want this man near me. This man's touch will not make me a woman.

THROUGH THE ACCORDION DOOR that served as a wall for 2 West, I picked up a note from a girl who'd been moved to 2 East. I was up and around by then. *Dear Daphne . . . The unit is much more like home than* three east and west. So far I really like it a lot. My first night hasn't been much different than two west though. Somebody hit one of the staff and tried to escape and there's this one guy who is totally freaked out who walks around and looks dumb and weird but other than that everything's been cool so far.

HEATHER WAS GETTING the boot from the hospital, too, I don't know why. In the lounge on 3 East and West we sat on the couch and browsed through pamphlets about long-term mental hospitals. The nurse said, "You two decide where you want to go."

Heather said, "You'd better go to the same place I'm going." It was like choosing colleges. We looked at the pictures in the brochures and tried to imagine being there, walking down that hill or across that lawn. We ruled out some places, like Menninger's in Topeka, Kansas, no way. In the brochure the Menninger buildings faced each other; you looked out of your window and saw another window, like a prison.

We liked the Constance Bultman Wilson Center for Adolescent Psychiatry in Faribault, Minnesota. The brochure made it sound like camp with an outdoor pool, tennis courts, a wooded bluff and a river. All teenagers, no adult patients. Plus it was kind of near Minneapolis. The big selling point was there were no fences so escape would be easier.

My father called the Wilson Center but they couldn't take me right away. Dr. Browning said she's got to go, now. My father got on the horn and called every hospital around Chicago. If I got discharged to home, my insurance would end. That would be it, no more. He dialed in a frenzy. Forest Hospital said sure, come on over. I had no idea what hospital I was going to until my father picked me up.

A few days before I was discharged, my father dropped off my suitcase so the staff let me go up to 3 East and West to pack, then I came back to seclusion on 2 West. Heather sent me a note in her bubble handwriting: *Dear Ducky, you better go to Wilson. I'm trying to get my parents to let me go. I want you to know that your so speicle.*

The seclusion room nurse said Kay was coming down from 3

East and West to say good-bye and I got in a panic. I didn't know how to say good-bye. I was sweating. I paced. Was I scaring Kay away by telling her I loved her and wanted her to be my mother? I couldn't help myself. No, I had to be cool. Did she even care about me half as much as I cared about her?

Somehow I said good-bye to her, but I don't remember it.

I rode the elevator up to the unit for a farewell. James wouldn't talk to me—he was so mad that I'd tried to kill myself. Danny stood around, not getting mushy. Everyone was the same, Jesus pacing, Jimi Hendrix roaming around, the anorexics reading copies of *Cosmo*. When they looked at me they weren't thinking, Lucky dog. They knew I wasn't getting out.

My father was waiting. The nurse brought me out of seclusion into the lobby, like a piece of luggage being moved.

TEN

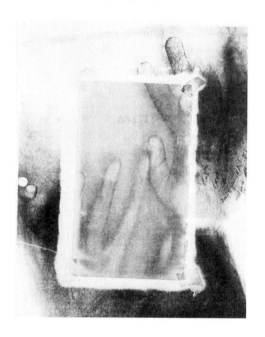

Forest Hospital
Des Plaines, Illinois
Admission: 2:15 p.m.
PSYCHIATRIC EVALUATION
DATE: 4-2-82
I. PRESENTING COMPLAINTS OR
PROBLEMS:
Patient is a 15 year old white female
who is being transferred here from
Michael Reese Hospital where she has
been hospitalized for the past 7 months
because of depression, substance abuse,
running away, lying and stealing.
II. DESCRIPTION OF PRESENT ILLNESS
(Include date of onset):

Patient states she has always had a number of problems because of her feeling that she was abused as a child and hates her father. Parents apparently are separated for a number of years and her mother has been unwilling to accept custody of the patient. She states she cannot relate to her father and constantly argues with him and fights with him all the time. She states she was doing poorly in school and was also abusing drugs and alcohol. She states she started drinking at age 7 and began using drugs at age 10. Prior to being hospitalized she states she was using drugs on a daily basis and after hospitalization went into withdrawal. She states she had lost control of her use of drugs and alcohol and had been in trouble in school because of her coming into school drunk. During her stay at Michael Reese the patient was not able to respond to the treatment given to her, she was quite resistant, angry and continued to be depressed. She states that while in the hospital she was able to use drugs and was taking a sleeping pill at night. Patient states that she has had numerous blackouts and still intends on abusing drugs and alcohol.

III. PAST HISTORY (Include individual, family, educational, vocational and social data):

Patient presently lives with her father, his girlfriend. There is a sister who is living with the mother. There is a grandfather who is described as being alcoholic on the mother's side. Patient is presently a freshman in high school and had been doing poorly in school for a number of years. Patient states that she was physically abused as a child, father denies this occurring and it has not occurred in some time since the patient has reached puberty. The patient states that a couple of years ago she had to go to work in order to support her mother because her mother was laid off from work.

IV. MEDICAL HISTORY AND CURRENT MED STATUS:

Patient has had the usual childhood illnesses and immunizations and is presently in good physical condition.

V. MENTAL STATUS: Include: General appearance and behavior; cognitive functioning (orientation, memory, general information, abstraction, concentration); thought processes and content (abnormal associations, homicidal and suicidal ideation); affect (intensity, fluctuations and liability, appropriateness); judgment/insight and description of patient's assets.

Patient is a well nourished white female who appears well oriented with an intact memory. She tends to present herself in a tomboyish manner but there is no evidence of any abnormal associations, homicidal or suicidal ideation at this time. Patient's affect is very depressed, she was tearful through most of the interview and was frequently quite hostile and angry. Patient's judgment is poor, she appears to lack any insight into her illness. At this point it is difficult to see any assets that might be present.

I LIKED TO THINK I was smarter than the doctors. I knew my own thoughts, inside my brain, and I knew what the doctors said about me and I felt smug because they couldn't tell a lie from the truth. On the other hand, I gave myself away—crying with Nurse Kay, for instance, and pleading for her to adopt me. But these moments were gaps: psychic leakage. Mostly I liked to be in control, to keep what was inside my brain inside. It was the only form of privacy I had left.

My lies were like a code language. When I told the counselor at Forest Hospital that before my stay at Michael Reese my use of cocaine had grown wild, I was testing him. The test was in two parts: a.) what will it take for you to pay attention to me, and b.) how gullible are you? He passed part a by writing furiously on a pad of paper about my daily use of cocaine and moving on to questions about other drugs: LSD? Speed? Alcohol? Heroin? To which I replied, *yeah, yeah, yeah,* except for heroin. I explained to him—his face has slipped from my memory but not his easy voice, the way he coaxed answers out of me, ready to believe the worst—I explained how my fear of needles would never let me flirt with heroin.

Part b he flunked. He was exceedingly gullible. But here was the catch. Bragging about drug use to an admissions counselor at a hospital that housed, in addition to a nut ward, a drug and alcohol re-habilitation unit—*we get results,* the advertisement said—was like making a bomb joke at the airport. *Doesn't that blow dryer in my suitcase look like a bomb in the x-ray? Ha, ha.* The system reacted and once acti-vated it could not be stopped. Which was how I ended up in rehab.

Rehab had several things going for it. First off, drug users were chic, far more chic than mental patients. Secondly, my non–drug problem was a major distraction from the topic I was anxious to avoid—the gender screw-up Dr. Browning told me I'd had since third grade. This played into my theory that I was smarter than the doctors; I had outwitted them again.

But the main appeal of rehab rested in the fact that I wanted to be a drug addict. Even as I lied about getting high, *yeah, yeah,* black-outs, *yeah, whatever,* I wished it were true. Drug addiction offered it-self to me like a blanket of forgiveness. *It's a disease. It's not my fault.* My parents, too, would be absolved of blame. We'd have something to tell ourselves and the world that seemed a lot more understandable than *my daughter won't wear a dress, my mother doesn't want me around, my fa-ther beats me, she's plain out of control, I don't know why I stole the money.*

If I weren't an addict, I figured I could act the part.

My father agreed to rehab since he almost believed the lies I told him. Before I went to Michael Reese, when things got dull around the house, I'd tell my father I'd just had a drug flashback, ants were crawling all over the bedspread, couldn't you see them? My father would say, Stop it, you're just trying to get attention, but I could tell he was unnerved.

He drove me from Michael Reese to Forest Hospital, forty-five minutes on the highway, flat out in the Cutlass, an afternoon off work for him, which he was none too happy about. I was sorry he had to take time off from work but not too sorry; I was the one who had to stay at a hospital tonight while he got to go home. We barely spoke. In the passenger seat of the Cutlass I jiggled my foot and stared out the window and tried not to think about being the biggest reject in mental hospital history.

A chirpy woman at the front desk shook my father's hand. "We'll take care of her," she said. My father and I said good-bye and for a second he looked at his feet, dejected. We didn't hug; he wasn't the huggy type, at least not with me. The chirpy woman gave me a brochure: *Welcome to Manor House. We hope your stay with us will be personally rewarding.*

The rooms were cozier than at Michael Reese, with carpeting and brown paneling on the walls like a redone basement. I sat on my bed and stared at the plywood, following the grain up and down with my gaze. Staring is a lot like taking drugs, you see patterns you'd never noticed, curled-up lips and ears, and there's something exciting about this, you want to tell someone, but part of you knows better. After I'd stared for a while I bit my nails. I chewed to the point where I exposed the soft pink flesh that was never meant to be uncovered. Painful, but also weirdly soothing. It was my pain, I caused it.

Two books lay on my nightstand: *Go Ask Alice* and *Alcoholics Anonymous*, which Ms. Chirpy called "the Big Book." I didn't bother with reading. My head was so full of thoughts I couldn't stuff any more inside.

I must have had a roommate but her name and face have disappeared from my mind.

Time passed: how much? In rehab they don't like you to be by yourself—*an addict alone is in bad company*. So it was probably a brief amount.

A knock on the door. This was already an improvement over Michael Reese, where no one knocked because the doors were always open. A fit-looking woman entered, strong arms, an asset to any softball team. Her name was Betty, she was a counselor, she was here to help. My mind clicked, sizing her up. From the delicate watch on her wrist I gathered she'd come from money.

She slid a straight-backed chair from the corner of the room to the edge of my bed. Eye contact: very important in rehab. She asked, "Do you feel you are worth getting better?"

Counselors, doctors: They are not interested in what you think. They want you to give them the right answer so they can walk away smiling, pleased at the progress they have instigated.

I wouldn't give the right answer.

"I don't know," I said. With my legs hanging over the side of the bed, I tapped the wall-to-wall carpet with my sneakers. "Not really."

She didn't flinch, her eyes—pale blue? hazel?—drilled into me. "Do you think you are worth getting better?"

The counselors were dense this way: everything was yes or no. How could I explain that my mind whirled around the phrase "getting better"? If I needed to get better, was that admitting that I was sick? If so, what sickness did I have? It wasn't drug addiction, although I couldn't blame Betty for not knowing that—I was sitting on a twin bed in Room 105 on a rehab unit—but since I knew I wasn't an addict maybe she was saying I was sick in a general way, as in mentally ill. I'd been through that question at Michael Reese, and ever since my sense of sanity had skidded around—although I'd never say this or she'd send me away. Michael Reese wouldn't have me so I'd be stuck at a state hospital where the lunatics rub their shit on the walls. I'd heard about this from Jesus, who'd been there and breathed the stench.

Betty stared at me and I stared at her. I said nothing. If my sickness wasn't mental illness I wondered if it was tied to my badness and the fact that I did not choose to wear a dress and that Dr. Browning said I was not an appropriate female.

All this whirly thinking in the blink of an eye.

Betty repeated the question.

Better to be a good patient. Better not to think. I said, "Yeah."

This wouldn't satisfy her. I had to repeat the sentence—*I believe I am worth getting better*—like a simpleton. She smiled. We were moving forward. She told me to repeat this first thing in the morning and before I went to sleep and whenever my motivation slackened. I said I would but inside I knew I'd never say the words out loud. Talking to myself made me feel crazy. I didn't want anything to do with it.

As she stood she suggested that I leave the past behind. I wanted to say, You don't know the half of it, but this is called arrogance and is not allowed in rehab: We have all suffered and our pain is equal. Try letting go, she said, but how could I when the past had me tight in its fist? She said good-bye and left me on my bed and I wanted to barricade the door and hide like Jean and Pudgy but I couldn't say this, either.

THE TRUTH WAS I'd tried cocaine with my Disciples gang friends—
I had tried quite a few things, but mostly I didn't have the energy to
chase down the drugs and snort, smoke or swallow them. They
weren't worth it to me. I'd never taken a drug that had sent me far
enough from my whirly thoughts to make me fall in love with it. Instead, pot made me paranoid and cocaine produced a nice tingle in
my head but nothing that said, This will make you whole. Also,
waiting for the effect to wear off made me nervous. Being high felt
as if half of me was wandering lost in the streets and half of me was
calling out, hoping that I'd make it back before someone took ad-
vantage.

A counselor handed me a list of rules. Rock-band tee shirts and
torn-up jeans were forbidden as were headbands, which were no
loss since I'd never liked the way they looked on me. In crafts we were
not allowed to print "Get High" or "Party Hardy." I couldn't resist
stamping "Dope" on a leather bracelet, which was immediately confiscated. We couldn't listen to our own music since rock bands
tended to glorify altered states of consciousness.

Smoking was the sole sanctioned vice. We could smoke at A.A.
meetings—and we did, whether we felt like it or not. We could also
smoke at the top of the hour for ten minutes in the lounge, a square
room with a lot of windows that were never opened.

This kind of smoking restriction really ups the urge to smoke.
None of us were what you might call in control of our impulses to
begin with. Hospital regulations also forbade coffee, caffeinated tea
and cookies or cakes sweetened with sugar—anything that gave a
nice rush to the nervous system. So by the time the anointed smoking period arrived we were a jittery crowd of about twenty.

We lined up to take a turn at the lighter—a heat coil mounted
in the wall, recessed inside a box the size of a light switch. You
leaned forward and pressed a button on top, which made the coil
turn red-hot. When it was my turn I pressed the button and let a few
people light their cigs. I could be friendly that way. Then I lit my
own, sending that first sweet flush of nicotine into my blood. Kiss-

ing the wall, we called it. *I've got to go kiss the wall.* The staff turned on an air-suck fan but the fan was unreliable and sometimes left a smoky blue haze that burned my eyeballs and coated my tongue. By the top of the hour the last wisp had drifted away and we'd line up to kiss the wall again.

This was our entertainment.

On the unit I was the youngest patient; I preferred being older than the others so I could dispense advice. My career goal was: *to become a musician long enough to support me through college and then a psychiatrist.* The psychiatrists I'd seen were inspiring in their ineptitude; surely, I could do better than them. Still, nobody on the unit wanted to hear my advice but many people had suggestions for me.

For our A.A. meeting, we sat in a circle in the lounge. My seat was a secretarial chair with metal legs. We spoke in turn and because of nervousness I could barely manage *My name is Daphne,* and everybody waited for me to add *I'm an alcoholic and a drug addict* but I didn't. I could lie to the doctors but not to the other patients, especially this group, a bunch of wrecks who were trying to own up to their diseases.

I remember one woman—middle-aged, curly-haired, regretful. She talked about her DUIs and how hard it was to stay clean and when she said the word *cocaine* it was as if the drug had been her best friend and lover. This started a debate in my head. Did I love cocaine? It was nice enough. I liked it. Did I love it? If I loved it, I'd fit in, I'd be part of the group. I wanted to love it. I wanted to, but the answer came back, No.

People were not supposed to glorify their drug use so she always added a negative twist—*it ruined everything.* What saved her was her higher power. *I get dressed and God does the rest.* I thought, Spare me. When I was younger we'd gone to a Lutheran church because my father had once dreamed of wearing the long black robe of a pastor. Walking down the aisle I'd held hands with my grandmother because I was her favorite and afterward she'd buy me a root beer float but in the church the prayers didn't mean anything. I mouthed the words but I wouldn't say them. My grandmother prayed beside me, her head of super-coarse gray hair tilted down. She told me, God will help you, have faith, but I didn't know what she was talking about.

The older I got the worse the fights became about whether I would wear a dress on Sunday. Then my mother moved out and going to church gave way to watching television. My mother would not set foot in a Catholic church, the church of her father; she said she was an agnostic so that's what I said I was, too.

Still, this woman with the higher power, her face lit up when she talked. It lit up. I couldn't ignore this. Envy shot through me; it was not her God I wanted, it was her hope. She believed her life could get better. Everyone clapped when she said how long she'd been clean and sober—it wasn't a long time, either, maybe two weeks. I thought, Jeez, I'm not an addict and no one's proud of me, no one's clapping.

As far as I could tell, I was the only higher power who'd ever taken an interest in my fate.

Each person in the group said something except for me. My silence became noticed. About halfway through the meeting I started to think, I've got to talk. Today, I've got to talk. Fear racked me so bad that sweat ran down my sides. I thought, After the curly-haired woman stops talking I'll raise my hand. A man with a cocky smile told the curly woman that her story was nothing compared to his, he'd been passed out cold from heroin and God knows what, and I wanted to tell him to quit glorifying himself. I was just about to say the words, a few faces turned toward me as if they could sense my imminent speech, when a man across the circle interrupted.

The opportunity passed; what I wanted to say wouldn't fit now. I tilted on the back two legs of the chair and waited for my desire to speak and be noticed and be part of the group to travel back through my nervous system. Up the synapses condemnation rushed: Why couldn't I spit something out like a normal person?

Once a week we piled into a convoy of white vans like prison inmates on an outing. We drove to an A.A. speaker's meeting at a church basement. Always there was a refreshment table off to one side where I could gulp a cup of coffee just to be a sneak and jam packets of sugar into my pockets so I could pour them later into my pathetic Manor House peppermint tea. Being a sneak was a diversion to keep myself afloat because listening to the A.A. stories was like taking on heavy water until I might sink. The room was smoky

and hot and one woman stood up and said she'd been in love with
the bottle for years which made her parents sick with grief and
worry. Nevertheless she couldn't stop until one day she drove down
the road, drunk as a fool behind the wheel, and hit a child riding a
bicycle. The child died. I thought, My God, I can't stand it. In my
mind I clearly saw the child on the road, stretched out dead with a
roundish face and wide blue eyes like Jean's. This woman stood up
front, sorry of course, but alive and proud to be sober. No sooner
did she sit down than another woman started to talk and we could
hardly understand her because of her sobs. The room was thick
with misery and hearing their sadness made me think of Anne over
at Michael Reese screaming about the Cornings coming and the
woman who had mush fed to her in tubes and it was too much. I felt
the badness inside me and wished I could confess to stealing the box
of Bubble Yum from the 7-Eleven and walking into people's houses
to take the change on the bureau and slapping my home ec teacher
across the face but I didn't have the drugs to blame so what was the
explanation? It must be my nature and I was doomed.

One guy on the unit, he'd had the usual trouble with cocaine and
whiskey and it had left him kind of mean, or maybe he'd been mean
before his troubles, he turned to me at our A.A. group and said how
much it ticked him off that I never spoke. He was twenty-five,
twenty-six, which to me seemed old, and he viewed himself as superior, I could hear it in his tone. He asked me if I thought I wasn't
an alcoholic.

Everyone looked at me. I couldn't look at the group or my
tongue would thicken so I focused on his eyes, but not exactly—
really I looked over his shoulder.

"I'm not an alcoholic," I said. To which he replied in a voice of
contempt that I was in denial.

"No, I'm not," I said, but it's hard to prove you're not a drunk
when you're already in rehab. I told him to work his own program
and stay out of mine.

The staff had a word for my denial: "massive."

A voice inside pipes up when you've made a mistake. A question
is raised—what am I doing here?—for which it is difficult to provide an answer. In my case, I pushed the question down by staring,

nail-biting and kissing the wall, but the question piped up again. I noted several facts: I was the youngest on the unit, I was not a drug addict or an alcoholic, and no one here was having fun. The strange quiet, compared to the racket I was used to, gave me plenty of room to examine these facts. The place needed a few good screamers. My days at Michael Reese started taking on a nostalgic tinge, which embarrassed me—I was lonely for a mental hospital. I missed Nurse Kay's smile and Heather writing me notes and Danny's deep voice singing a Luther Vandross ballad. I missed Jesus and his lengthy planning for his apostles' reunion. At least it was amusing. At least they'd liked me.

I didn't make a friend on the unit. I was friendly with a couple of people, but I didn't meet anyone I kept in touch with. I'd sit at meals with the other patients and keep my head down and look at my tray. From across the cafeteria one night I heard a guy say how everyone was working their programs, trying to save their necks, except for Daphne, who thinks she doesn't have a problem. Another guy says, Oh, yeah, Daphne, what's wrong with her? I wolfed my Swiss cheese sandwich and glass of milk and fled to my bed.

Sleep. I got good at sleep. Talk about a drug.

Later in the week I pulled aside a counselor named Edith, who wore her blond bangs straight across her forehead, and asked her to meet me in my room. Sitting down face-to-face I explained that I'd made up my drug history to get attention from my parents. I told her I had never and did not now have a problem with drugs and alcohol and I would sure appreciate it if she could do something about getting me off this unit. I knew the hospital wouldn't let me out into the world. That was fine by me. I just wanted off this unit.

She said I needed to work on getting honest with myself.

"Flat affect" my counselors called my mood, which was explained to me as the absolute lack of emotion. This had been my facial expression for some time but in rehab the counselors kept after me about it. They gave me a yellow sheet of paper with a list of feelings to circle. I skipped over hope, joy, love and anything else positive. The ones I circled were: *lonely, angry, unloved, puzzled, disgusted, defeated, rejected*—I wrote in *hopeless* since it wasn't on the list.

I handed in my sheet and the counselor looked it over and now she knew my insides so she had one up on me. She said, *Being honest is the first step in healing* and I kept my face as blank as a little white pill. I didn't know what I wanted her to say about *lonely, angry, unloved* and so on but this was my heart and what I wanted was more than she said and perhaps more than any one person could say.

A couple of times I used the phone in the lounge to call over to Michael Reese—for me, it was calling home. When you feel mis-understood, you go to the last place you felt misunderstood to get comfort. I talked to Bertha, the older woman who answered the phone on 3 East and West. "Everything's pretty much the same," she'd say. I liked hearing her voice but I couldn't say I wanted to come back; I didn't really.

FAMILY THERAPY was down the hall and around the corner, in the office of the therapist, a woman who wore fashionably tinted glasses that made her eyes look shadowy. Family therapy was an overstate-ment; it was my mother and me in two chairs with the therapist in her chair across the room. Or sometimes it would be my father, his girlfriend and me; my mother and father didn't meet with me at the same time.

My mother was already in her chair when I came into the room; I shot her a cold look. Hugs were out of the question; my mother had stopped hugging Jean and me a long time ago. As soon as I sat down my mother said I was a great disappointment, she didn't un-derstand why I had to be so disruptive to the family, and I said, I'm just as disappointed in you. The conversation was the same every time. Then the therapist woman interrupted to give her opinion, which is what the insurance company was paying her to do.

Shifting in her chair a quarter-turn to face my mother she said, "It seems to me Daphne is looking for a mother. Is there enough room in your life for a mother-daughter relationship?"

My mother said, "No."

I stared at the wall, which was white without a swirly ear or lip like the paneling in my room but that was okay because even though I was staring at the wall I couldn't really see it.

I wouldn't cry in front of my mother, I wouldn't cry, and even lying in my bed at night my eyes stayed dry.

EDITH, the counselor with the bangs, hammered me about my denial and suggested I write a paper on "honesty with oneself." This made my stomach feel as if someone had wrapped cellophane around it. Everything tight.

I had glimmers. Sparks of thoughts quickly stamped out. The Little League boys yelled, tomboy, tomboy, and they were jerks but something sparked inside me. Dr. Browning peered through his glasses and said I was not appropriate and I hated him but— I don't know—I did feel kind of different. Sometimes I remembered the roller-skating rink and a pretty girl—not one in particular, a blend of them all—her hair flying loose and the tingle in my stomach.

If anyone found out I liked to roller-skate with a girl I'd be locked up in the psycho ward forever, which I was probably going to be, anyway.

I'd been writing down anything that flew through my head ever since my last class at Rolling Meadows High School. We got half a credit for keeping a journal; mine was a spiral notebook with F.T.W. on the front for Fuck The World. The teacher would read my journal and write back and mostly I was pretty honest. I liked the teacher, her name was Linda. When I wrote that my father and I weren't talking ever since he found out I cut class and he threw me around my room, she wrote, *Sounds like things are bad for you at home.*

Now for a journal I had a black binder and loose-leaf paper. I pulled out the binder from under my pillow and lay on my stomach on my bed.

11 p.m. This place is driving me crazy. I've confessed to my lies and I've tried to be as honest as possible and I'm still catching hell for it. Why don't people forgive me? I've finally after all these years been able to tell someone I was lying and I felt really good after I let that out but now I feel just as bad because people won't believe me.

I'm being as honest as I ever have been. I'm tired of fucking myself over. I'm not going to lie anymore. I don't want attention from parents . . . I'm not going to play the game the way they want me to. . . .

p.s. I think I like girls.

Four days later Dr. Abdullah, my psychiatrist, said to me, "I've come to realize you have a sexual problem." He spoke with authority; it was a declaration.

We were sitting in his office, a cluttered room the size of a closet. With his black hair and accent, Dr. Abdullah reminded me of Mahmoud, my mother's boyfriend, which was not a happy association. His words stunned me. For a giddy moment, I thought, *Funny, I was just thinking the same thing.*

Dr. Abdullah's head tilted down but at the same time he kept his eyes on me, as if he was looking out of the top of his skull. I've seen other doctors do this. It's a way they can look down at you even when you're sitting at their level.

I kept a tremble out of my voice; from years of practice I managed a tough look on my face. "What do you mean?"

"Do you like girls?" he asked. Dr. Abdullah was a man of short sentences. He'd comment and I'd comment back. Our sessions had a staccato rhythm.

I gave my most casual reply. "Sure."

"How do you like girls?"

"They're good friends."

"I see." He drummed his left fingers, pinkie to forefinger, on his metal desk. A pause, then a trace of hopefulness in his voice: "Are you attracted to boys?"

Psychiatrists are so often stupid. My soul was right under my shirt, begging to be seen, and he would rather not look; his fear of what might be hidden surpassed my fear, which was considerable. I took the power he handed me: who wouldn't? Any girl child knew the right answer to his question.

"Yeah," I said.

The tension lifted. My answer made him feel better, which seemed to be the point; psychiatrists do not like to be unsettled.

"You're a pretty girl," he said. With improved grooming—good hygiene, he called it—I could build my confidence around boys.

He would help me; it seemed clear to him that I liked boys but by the looks of me, I didn't know how to attract them.

"Have you considered styling your hair?" he asked.

I nodded like an idiot. Relief trickled through me, but from what? That I had fooled him? In part, but this also was true: Like him, I wanted to erase the words I'd written in my journal. I thought if I could avoid talking about the tingle in my stomach when I roller-skated with a pretty girl—if I could avoid this long enough the tingle might disappear.

He said, "I'll see you at our next appointment," which was my signal to leave. I didn't look at him as I exited but I felt his gaze upon my shirt—a boyish black tee shirt hanging out of my jeans; I knew that now I'd have to hear his opinion about what I wore.

More than ever Dr. Abdullah was my enemy, but not a clearly defined enemy, because I flipped back and forth, a little bit of me wanting to believe that he could make me into a girly-girl which would be a relief because I wanted to be called normal and I knew I must look unspeakably awful the way I was because I'd been told so for years. At the same time I hated him. He was a coward when what I needed was a brave heart to inspire my own.

AFTER LEAVING Dr. Abdullah's office, I walked diagonally across the hall to the wooden front desk. I didn't give Dr. Abdullah credit for reaching his conclusions about my sexual problem; I wanted to see who on the staff had given him a clue.

Reaching over the edge of the counter I rummaged around until I found my chart which was kept on a metal clipboard of the sort doctors carry around. On one edge of the clipboard was an opening that slid up and down to let the staff know if the patient had been charted—if the opening showed fluorescent blue it meant one thing and fluorescent orange meant another. As patients, we were entitled to read our charts at any time. At Michael Reese we couldn't, but here we could. Sometimes I read my chart every day to keep tabs on what the counselors were saying about me: *She gave clear, concise feedback abt. peers, but seems to lack insight into her own problems.*

I hadn't read my chart in a while.

I undid the red Velcro band that kept the chart together and flipped up the pages until I came to what I was looking for. What I found wasn't a standard charting form—it was a scrap of paper stuck in my record. On it were words written in scrawly handwriting—whose? A note that said the patient was struggling with identity issues. Evidence for this was given in a quote: "p.s. I think I like girls."

They had read my journal.

They had gone into my room when I was off somewhere—maybe in the classroom down the hall where seven or eight of us from all over the hospital sat in cubicles facing the wall and worked on math or English, moving at our own pace, as the kindly teacher put it. Or maybe I'd been in the shower, with the hot water beating on my face, pretending I was outside in the rain—the desire to be outside, alone, was like a hunger in me.

They'd gone into my room and searched for my black binder in the top drawer in the nightstand or under my pillow and put their hands on the cover. Paged through it.

Holding the chart in my hand, I had to contain myself. I had to think this through.

I walked back to my room and sat on my bed. I couldn't deny I'd written the words. It was too late for that. My mind flipped all over the place. *I'm fucked, I'm fucked. They've found me out. They have something on me now.* What I wanted to do was sleep, I was so tired, but I was on the shit list now so when it was time for my afternoon goals group, I attended. After group I kissed the wall and pretended everything was fine.

No plan emerged. I returned to the front desk. One of the counselors was there, maybe Betty, I can't remember exactly. I picked up my chart and pointed to the quotation.

"Where did this come from?" I asked. My voice was not nasty, I didn't dare. The counselor recited the official policy: "Anything we have access to, any notes or anything you've written, can be used in your treatment plan unless it is specifically marked not to be used."

On the top of a clean page of my journal I wrote: IF FOUND

NOT TO BE CHARTED. LEAVE ME ALONE YOU ASS-HOLES.

In my next journal entry I wrote that I wanted to die and this was not girlish exaggeration although swallowing the Sea Breeze and the lighter fluid had taken away my desire for the suicidal act. What I wanted now was to not wake up, to be passively removed, to be sucked out of the air like the smoke in the lounge.

4/20/82 Pt. Appeared angry during third hour class. She swore repeatedly and made numerous negative comments re school. In fifth hour class pt. refused to respond to teacher's questions re school work. She stared into space with legs in constant motion. When asked if she wished to discuss what was bothering her, pt. said, "no."

——, Teacher

4/23/82 (3-11) Daphne attended Dr. ——'s group today. She was encouraged to attend 7 p.m. group and did so. However, she did not participate at all in discussions although she did appear to listen intently. She appears preoccupied and much more quiet than usual. Hygiene poor and her appearance is unkempt. Appears depressed. Remains alone much of the shift.

——, R.N.

Dr. Abdullah might have sent the counselor to see me in my room, or maybe she came on her own. Her name was Erica, she had long dark feathered hair, super feminine, and when she walked in I was sitting in bed with my back against the wall, staring at the paneling. She said she wanted to talk and I knew what subject she had in mind. She said this was a time of confusion for me and getting my feelings out in the open would help. I didn't trust her one bit.

I said, "It started when I was born. My parents wanted a boy so they tried to raise me that way."

She looked concerned. I continued.

"My parents made me play Little League and never let me dress like a girl."

A frown creased her face. She made sympathetic murmuring noises.

I nodded. "This confused me a lot," I said.

For the record, I wrote the conversation word for word in my journal.

THIS NEW ATTENTION seized up my stomach. After dinner in the cafeteria—Swiss cheese and tomato on white, tons of mayo, and a pale cookie that tasted lemony instead of sweet—I didn't feel well. In my bathroom I closed the door for a moment of privacy, kneeled down and threw up in the toilet and wished every feeling I had inside would come out of me for good. A counselor passing by stood and listened to my retching. It's the kind of thing counselors do in rehab: listen at bathroom doors. She said she wondered why I was throwing up my dinner and her gaze traveled over my body to see if I was too fat or too thin. I asked, "Why were you listening?" She scurried back to the front desk to write it all down and in her excitement she gave me an idea of how I could have a normal problem, like everyone else, and not an issue about pretty girls and a tingling sensation.

4-27-82 (7-3) Staff talked 1:1 with Daphne. Daphne openly admits she is anorexic and that she eats once a day & vomits afterward. She told staff she doesn't feel this is a problem but was encouraged by staff to talk to Dr.——.

———, P.A.

My sessions with Dr. Abdullah were like a game of Battleship—figuring out where his ships were and how to hide my ships. Every question was an attack I had to deflect.

For instance: He asked me, Were there any boys I was sweet on?

I ignored his question. I looked at him as if our previous conversation had never happened and said I'd been having a terrible time holding down food.

"Vomiting?" he asked.

"Yeah. I'm too fat."

He jotted something down in his notebook. I said the vomiting just happens, I don't induce it. He said we were finally battering down those intellectual defenses the doctors had taught me at Michael Reese. I didn't know what he was talking about but I was glad he was pleased.

He asked me how long the vomiting had been going on. I said, Oh, off and on for a long time, I guess, and he watched me in his tilty-head way, absorbing every word of our therapeutic breakthrough.

He said he wanted me to speak to Dr. Freeman on another unit since it appeared that other issues were more pressing right now than my drug and alcohol addictions.

I kept my gaze on the carpeting to hide my pleasure.

"Which unit?" I asked.

"Town House," he said. All the units had hokey names. One was called Country House. If you were sent there you could tell people, I've gone to the country house, and no one would be the wiser.

We never got around to talking about crushes on boys, our time was up.

ELEVEN

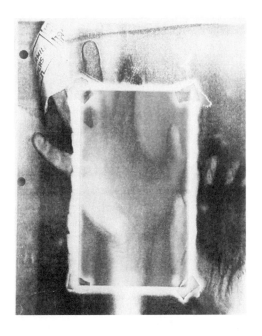

IN SEVENTH GRADE *the girls in my class*

developed a passion for makeup. On the morning bus

ride they'd apply the finishing touches to their

eyelids, keeping a steady hand despite the bumps

in the road. After gym class they'd stand all in a row

with their noses up to the mirror: blue eye shadow to

the brow, mascara clotted onto the lashes, pink frost

applied to the lips—done.

Two girls in my class were my friends, even though they were girly-girls and I wasn't. Michelle was my best friend, kind of slutty. We talked on the phone every night, her family was a wreck, father gone, mother dating like a fiend. But her mother was cool, too, because she let Michelle smoke in the house. Michelle had a friend, Linda, who was my friend through Michelle. Linda was heavyset with a reputation that a guy could get someplace with her. Drifting along with them was Barbara, a straggler in tight jeans.

They liked me because I liked getting into trouble. On the last day of school I'd be the one pushing open the emergency exit at the back of the bus so we could end the year in style.

After school most days we trailed off the bus at the same stop and headed for the park, where we climbed up the little kids' slide and sat in the dome at the top. Michelle, Linda and Barbara passed around a joint. I didn't partake. I smoked a Marlboro.

After a while Michelle said, "What would Daphne look like in makeup?" The idea struck Linda and Barbara as funny. Linda had a horrible ha-ha laugh, super fake, and when she smiled her lips looked crooked and way too red. I smiled like someone trying to hold in a fart.

We slid down the slide and walked in the grass. From behind me Linda pushed me down, ha-haing as if it were a big joke. Barbara swung her tight-jean thighs and sat on my stomach. She held my wrists over my head.

They were girls, I couldn't punch them.

Linda opened her purse which was a wreck inside, torn-up Kleenex and lint in the crack of her lipstick case. She handed Michelle a compact of turquoise eye shadow, which Michelle applied with a heavy hand to my eyelids. From another compact she rubbed on blush across my cheeks thick as dust. Red lipstick she dabbed on fiercely. "Look at Daphne in makeup." All of them ha-haing like crazy. When Barbara took her hands off my arms, I squiggled free and ran off.

The park bathroom had a cement floor and a row of sinks. The mirror had little black flecks all over it, like fleas, but I could still see myself. I looked stupid, like somebody'd gone and stuck another face on me. I kept waiting to feel a pull, there you are, glamorous, older, prettier. Nothing. I splashed water on my face making a smeary mess.

Michelle came up behind me at the sink. From her purse she produced a jar of makeup remover, which I stuck my fingers into. I rinsed, but my face was still blurry red and turquoise.

When this makeup attack happened three times more, I couldn't pretend Michelle was my best friend, even though we still talked on the phone.

MY FATHER'S HOUSE had a sliding glass door looking out on the backyard. It was my stage. I dragged out the Hoover upright to use the handle as a stand-up microphone and turned on the stereo full tilt. 1:30 p.m. I should have been in school but I didn't want to get on the bus with those girls. I decided I'd practice for my career as a rock star, for which I didn't need Robert Frost Junior High.

I took the Hoover handle and sang "Only the Good Die Young" until I knew all the words. In some parts my voice was lower than Billy Joel's crooning; kids at school teased me about my low voice, what's with your voice, you sound like a guy, but my voice was a replica of my mother's. After a couple of times it grew dull to be singing to myself when I knew I was talented but no one else knew of my promising career. I didn't know who to sing to but I knew a number in the phone book that people could call if they were thinking about killing themselves. I'd looked up the number once when things were really bad, dialed one or two digits and hung up.

I called the number. I asked the counselor if I could sing for her and she said, "Sure"—what else could she say? I put the phone receiver on the rug and belted out the song and she said she liked it. I gave her an encore.

listening ears

JEAN AND I ran away for Mother's Day. My father wanted to go up to see his mother and we wanted to see our mother, but he said no. I said, "I'm leaving, I'm going," and Jean came with me out the back door. We went down the hill and stopped by Lisa's house to ask her if she wanted to go to Chicago. Lisa's father was mean and her family kept the shades down in the house, no light ever. If her father came home and I was over I'd have to climb out the window of her room.

Lisa said, Chicago sounds cool, but my father would kill me. We left without her. In Chicago Jean and I found the Sears Tower, took the elevator up and looked around at four states: Wisconsin, Michigan, Indiana and Illinois. All flat and neatly divided. Then we took the 'L' out to my mother's. "What are you doing here?" she said when she opened the door. "Happy Mother's Day," we said.

She called my dad and when we got home my father took me into his room, hit me with the belt, told me what we'd done was wrong, disrespectful. When he was finished, he said, "Send your sister in," and I said, "Over my dead body." "Now it's your sister's turn," he said, and I stood in front of him and said, "You're going to have to kill me first," so he gave up the idea.

FIRESIDE: *the largest operating roller-skating rink in the world. Dangling over the center of the rink was a silver disco ball. On the side was a place to get a greasy hot dog or a wad of cotton candy. I went by myself, although some kids I knew were there. But a lot of kids came from all over, the other towns.*

With the lights lowered, the announcer came on and said the next skate was couple skate. I hung back in a sick dread and looked at my feet in the white rental skates with red wheels. I knew what would happen. Sure enough a girl rolled up to me and asked would I like to skate.

I had a couple of choices, none of them good.

Al Green's voice came over the loudspeakers singing a slow, sexy song, and the girl looked at me wondering why I didn't speak so I choked out "Nah, I don't feel like it," and shook my head. I couldn't look at her for shame.

A bunch of loud-mouthed boys stared at me and figured it out and said what the hell was I trying to do by passing myself off as a boy. The girl and her friends turned evil and when I went into the bathroom a group of them followed me in and said, "Are you sure you're a girl?" Sitting in the stall, I waited until their laughing stopped and I heard the door close behind them.

A couple of times when the girl seemed nice I skated with her, our arms interlocked, our legs moving in synch on the shiny wood. Leaning into the turns, I wished I could do a cross-over with my skates, to show off. It was fun, I felt puffed up and taller. The girls were pretty with their long hair flowing behind them. Seeing them up close, their fuzzy sweaters and the way they moved their legs, made my stomach tingle and I thought, I shouldn't be feeling this, and then the thought fell out of my mind. As soon as I stepped off the rink it was as if skating with the pretty girl had never happened. Except I had the urge to do it again. Every time I skated with a girl it was new.

More than once the girl found out later that I was a girl. One time she told a guy who rolled over and said, "What do you think you're doing?"

I said, "Are you going to hit a girl?" And I shoved him. "Are you going to hit a girl?" I said, because I knew he wouldn't, and shoved him again.

They got to be afraid of me. All you have to do is look a little bit like a boy and they think you're a crazy girl who's going to rip their heads off and spit down their necks.

After a while I stopped going to the rink which was okay with my father since he didn't have to drive me anymore but he wished I'd keep myself busy. He didn't like feeling that he should think something up for me to do. I stepped outside and played with the younger kids on the block. Even though I was too old for tag, it wasn't bad—I always won.

MRS. LANGLEY said now class we'll be working on pillows shaped in the letter of your names, first or last, you choose. Each girl is to bring in a yard of fabric, a roll of color-coordinated thread, a packet of needles and stuffing. Do you understand?

I did. I'd wanted to take shop because I liked to build boxes and lamps but I was shuttled into home ec with no chance to argue and there was no way in hell I'd be able to get the fabric or the stuffing because my father would never get around to taking me to the store.

My friends let me borrow a needle and a spool of thread and bits of extra fabric. I was going to make a patchwork D. Mrs. Langley circulated among the round tables checking each girl's progress and when she stood over me I threaded the needle.

"What's this?" she asked, staring at the pile of fabric scraps. I told her my father wouldn't buy me fabric. She frowned. She said I had nothing I needed and if I didn't have a solid piece of fabric, not itty-bitty scraps, then I couldn't do the project. I told her it was unfair and she said she had one standard and it applied to everyone and why did I think I would be an exception?

I said, "Fine," and tossed the thread back to my friend Susan across the room. I chucked the thimble to Lorraine. The pack of needles to Brenda. The girls in the class moved back in their seats and Mrs. Langley walked from the front through the parting of the room.

"You're right," I told her. "I have nothing."

She asked was I ready to go to the principal's office and I said no.

She stood close enough for me to see the cracks in her lips where her pink lipstick was wearing off and I felt her black eyes seeing me as worthless trash. I rose from my seat. My hand lifted up and I slapped her cheek, not full force, but hard enough.

"Now I'm ready," I said.

Down the hall past the lockers, turn left, up the corridor, turn right into the principal's office, I walked cocky, running my hands along the padlocks on the lockers so they went bam-bam-bam against the metal. I liked putting fear in Mrs. Langley and anyone I could, but inside I thought, I'm a violent maniac just like my father.

JOEY, LUIS AND I faithfully attended homeroom at Sullivan High School, a huge brick school, then met on the concrete front steps. We walked over to Freedy's arcade, a dusty place jammed with video games, and played Asteroids. I'd be like a robot, my right hand on the attack button moving moving moving, attack, hit, the whoomp, whoomp sound like a siren coming out of the machine until I reached 999,999 and the numbers flipped back to zero.

When Joey needed a place to stay I let him live in my closet. It was narrow but deep, under the stairs in my mother's apartment. My mother slept upstairs; she didn't know he was there. One night someone knocked at the back door in the basement. I stood up in my sleeping bag and hopped to the door. It was Luis, all bloody. A Latin King had knifed him in the bicep. I called Joey out of the closet. Jean woke up, scared, but I told her don't worry, it's okay. I wrapped the cut in my old AC/DC tee shirt. Traveling by bus, we took Luis to the hospital and dropped him off. Joey and I went looking for the guy who'd stabbed him. They'd been fighting over a girl. We walked fast and hard like soldiers and asked a guy standing at the corner if he'd seen him. I felt safe, out with my brother, my family. The more we didn't find the Latin King, the braver I felt.

Jean told my mother, There's a boy living in the closet. My mother said, "Really? Show me." They opened the door and saw blankets and a pillow and Joey's crumpled clothes.

The weather was bitter, snowy, and my mother said Joey could stay here but he needed to sleep upstairs. So at night he'd take the cushions off the love seat and sleep on the living-room floor. One night he came home drunk and my mother said, That's it, you can't stay here. He moved to some relative's house.

When the weather got warm, a bunch of us started spending the night on the beach at Lake Michigan. One of the boys, Philip, liked me and so he was my boyfriend. He was so sad and depressed he wasn't that demanding. I kissed him a couple of times. His father was a politician, which put a lot of pressure on him; Philip had to wear a suit on Sunday and stand on the church steps and shake hands. A church woman leaned over to him and said, "I hear you're having a hard time, Philip." He'd never met her before in his life. Later he tried to commit suicide. At the beach we'd find a comfortable rock and lie down close together to stay warm. The lake water made a little sound, a steady hum.

My mother said she was at her wit's end with me, I was stealing her money and flunking school and provoking fights in the family, so we went to see a counselor at the Doyle Center at Loyola University, in our neighborhood. My mother told the counselor her strategy in dealing with me was to ignore my bad behavior and reward my positive behavior. Tough love, she called it. She said she woke up one day and realized it had been more than a year since she'd said anything positive to me.

When I was alone with the counselor I'd show up late and sit in the chair with my arms across my chest. I wasn't going to tell her anything.

Sometimes my dad and Jean came with my mom and me. The counselor said, "Let's pretend we're making a movie. Each of you act out the part you see yourself as." Jean said, "I feel like a speck of dust in the corner," and my mother started to cry.

I GOT KICKED OUT of Sullivan High School for threatening to blow up my math teacher's car. He'd made comments insulting my mother, so I'd retaliated, but my threat was idle. I wouldn't have done it.

The therapist said I should have a more disciplined environment, so I moved to my father's. I hated being away from my sister. When my parents split up, they said Jean and I would stay together, we'd at least have each other no matter where we were. But it didn't work out that way. I transferred to Rolling Meadows High School in Rolling Meadows, where my father had moved to a modern apartment complex with an artificial lake and tennis courts. He had a girlfriend he was serious about—Melanie. She had an apartment there, but they traded up to a two-bedroom. My father rented out the house in Roselle. My father said he and his girlfriend were my parents now and couldn't I be nice to her?

Melanie wasn't like my mother, who was super hip, and she wasn't like me. She wore nail polish and lipstick and took time styling her hair. She'd say, Why don't you try this blouse of mine, wouldn't it look pretty on you? And sometimes I'd try it on and my father would fall over himself with the compliments. She was trying to help but in a pink blouse with a Peter Pan collar, I looked like a dork, so I'd end up mad, which hurt her feelings.

All the furniture in the apartment was Melanie's, a glass dining-room table and a thick couch and love-seat combo, nicer than our old stuff, but I missed the orange carpet all matted down. When my father sat on the couch Melanie would sit on his lap and I'd have to leave the room. I'd never seen my father like this— affectionate. At night she'd stop by my room, stand in the doorway and ask, How are things going? I'd be sitting against the wall with my drawing board on my lap, my markers and pencils spread out on the bed. I'd move one side of my headphones off my ear and say, Fine. She knew she wasn't going to get anywhere with me. I felt sorry for her, having to deal with me when my behavior was kind of unraveling.

She couldn't understand why I didn't get along with my father. She looked at him and saw a guy who tickled her on the couch and I saw a guy who beat me with a belt until I stopped crying. So we were in two different movies.

My joining them was not viewed as an enhancement to their relationship. Melanie had a camera and she said I'd taken it, which I hadn't. Where is it, what have you done with the camera? She wasn't violent but she had a scream that went right through you. My father beat me a couple of days in a row. I broke into their room and found the camera exactly where it was supposed to be. I said, "Look in the closet, it's there." Melanie said, "You put it back."

When we ate pizza for dinner my jaw cracked. She said, "No one's going to love you if your jaw cracks at the table." I took a bite and my jaw cracked again. I couldn't help it.

During an in-school suspension at Rolling Meadows High my counselor made me take the Minnesota Multiphasic Personality Inventory. The test consisted of five hundred and fifty-six true/false questions. I still have a copy of it. The counselor called my father with the results. "Your daughter is out of control and has a criminal mind."

My father absolutely believed him. It was as if he'd never known me to be anything else.

The Doyle Center referred my family to the Northwest Mental Health Center. The therapist said, "We feel the best solution is to send Daphne away for long-term psychiatric treatment. You're losing your other daughter." My mother said, "What else can we do? I can't handle Daphne." My father said, "She's out of control."

When she found out I was leaving, Jean didn't say anything. She kept quiet so she wouldn't be sent away, too.

TWELVE

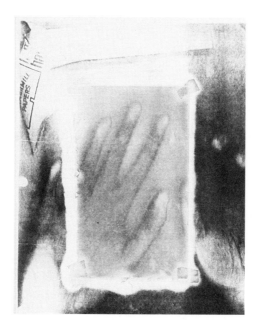

5/1/82 Daphne was transferred to T.H. at 1 p.m. Staff escorted her there w. all her belongings. She seemed in fair spirits, affect flat. She talked w. staff about feeling she would get the help she needed on the other unit as she didn't have a drug problem. She was encouraged to work while on the other unit.

———, P.A.

I said my good-byes in rehab without any boo-hoos. Most everyone thought I was a lying girl who could not face her addiction but at least they didn't know why I was being moved. If they knew about the vomiting, I didn't care, it was a game. As far as I could tell there were no rumors about my sexual problem.

I thought of my transfer as a victory and as I walked past the *One Day At A Time* poster on the wall near the front desk and the counselor dragging the chairs into a circle in the smoky lounge, I wanted to hiss, See, I told you I wasn't a drug addict.

Of course I didn't know what lay ahead. I thought it could be no worse than what I'd been through already. We always think that, I suppose. It is human nature to be optimistic about a change. The less we know about what lies ahead the more free we are to imagine that the next place will surely be an improvement, if not a refuge. This made my walk pleasant, down the hall, out the double doors, past the classrooms, through the metal door into Town House. It was the farthest I'd walked in the hospital, which in itself felt exciting, but the pleasantness dried up soon enough.

I'm a shifter, even now, and know how to move quickly from place to place and arrange my things so I have some order and feel a room is mine. I developed this habit traveling between my mother's and my father's and staking out a clearing in hostile territory. In my new room two girls lounged on their beds, the only empty bed was the top bunk which I knew was for me. The girl on the twin said her name was Donna, she wore blue eye shadow and her hair was permed in crinkly waves. On the lower bunk was Carol, who was kind of hyper with a jiggle in her foot, stick-straight hair and a brooding face. I didn't ask them directly what they were in for, not wanting to be rude, and I never did find out but I assume they were in for depression or family problems for which they were singled out as the cause.

They weren't shy with me and I was so happy to be away from the drug addicts that I felt chatty and told them about the guy who'd passed out on heroin and Donna seemed impressed so I left it a bit vague about what drugs I'd tried myself.

They filled me in on the Town House unit, which they said was not terrible. Donna said you will live or die by points—she was dramatic since she was aiming for an acting career. Points could be earned making your bed, washing your hair or role playing in group therapy, which Donna said meant acting like someone's abusive mother, screaming and yelling, which I was not looking forward to. Points add up to privileges and without points this place is a prison, Donna said, to which Carol added, It's a prison without M&M's, Snickers, or Bubble Yum. Sugar was banned, the staff feared it would make us excitable.

As far as points went I'd be starting out on Level 1 and what I wanted was Level 4, which meant outside privileges on the grounds. Over in rehab, I'd looked out the window and seen two lawn chairs and a table outside in a courtyard. I wanted to be able to sit on one of those chairs with the sun on my face and breathe air no one else had breathed. Anytime I'd go outside—to an A.A. meeting or to run around the lawn in a pathetic p.e. class—I never felt that I was outside. I couldn't feel the air on my skin. The attendants watched our every move; their eyes stole everything from me.

The kids at Town House were different from the kids at Michael Reese, they were suburban kids, well fed with shiny hair, no screamers or hallucinators. Twenty-three kids, plus me. In group therapy—points for attending, points for speaking—the topic came up of what you would do if you had freedom from your parents for one weekend. This girl named Shirley, a smart aleck, smirked and said she'd go wild with her friend Faye who knew how to party and also had her learner's permit. Nick, a young, stringy boy, said he'd skip school and take some money and, and, and, his stutter kicked up from the thrill of freedom and also from not wanting to say the wrong thing in front of the counselor.

I said, "I would like one weekend of structure from my parents."
Shirley said that was stupid.

I said I was sick of having to find my own food and sleeping under my friend's stairs because I hated my father and begging for change because I had no money. I could feel my face getting hot, which was as close as I got to crying, but when I looked around the group all the faces looked annoyed, except the counselor's, which looked confused.

After a pause Donna said she'd have a party like the one she'd gone to when her friend's parents were away, they'd unlocked the liquor cabinet and made rum-and-Cokes.

I didn't say anything else. Afterward I sat with Nick at supper. He was my buddy, eleven years old, Jean's age. I helped him with his homework and agreed to watch tv with him if he finished his spelling. Unless Nick went totally bonkers he'd have to go back to school in his neighborhood and listen to kids whisper that he'd been locked up for being crazy. This seemed to me the worst thing—to be locked up which was freaky enough, then to have to go back in the world to be tormented alone. At least I didn't have to worry about that since I was in for the duration, however long that would be, although I didn't tell this to Nick because I didn't want to make him feel bad.

We sat at a long table and I told Nick to drink his milk, he needed his strength, and he said I helped him more than any counselor, which made me feel good.

MY NEW PSYCHIATRIST had a full white beard and kind eyes that looked right at me. Dr. Freeman. I met with him in a conference room on the unit—one wall was glass but not many people walked by to look in. After initial formalities about how I was adjusting to the unit, he asked me was I eating all right? And I said yes, I felt better here, my eating was fine, and he seemed pleased.

He said, "I understand you spoke with Dr. Abdullah about identity issues and sexual confusion."

His eyes were so kind, they were blue I think. I thought he could help me. I said, "I don't know if I like boys or girls."

He nodded his head and kept silent so I said I felt mixed up and depressed and the problem had been weighing on my mind a long time.

He said, "We'll make up a treatment plan to set you on the right track," and this sounded good to me. I wanted to be on the right track, a place I'd never been.

He said his initial impression was that the root of my depression was the poor treatment I'd received from my parents and my peers—

he used that word, peers, instead of friends—and I thought, Yes, it's true.

Then he said in the same friendly voice that if I appeared more feminine I would be better adjusted. With a neater look, people would treat me in a different way, he said. He smiled. He truly believed he was helping me.

Our time was up and I stood up kind of shaky. Even this man with the kind blue eyes wanted me to cover my face with makeup. The bruises underneath my skin—didn't he want to put his finger lightly on each one and say, Tell me about it?

I MET with Dr. Freeman again. I didn't wait for him to steer the conversation, I launched into my fear of water, which was as great as my fear of needles. I told him that when I was seven years old I went to a neighborhood pond with a friend and the friend fell in and I tried to save him but he fell so deep. All I could see was his hair floating up in the dark water which was green with algae so no light could shine through it. He sank to the bottom and disappeared. I said I blamed myself and ever since have felt my pulse beat fast when I'm near a pond or even a chlorinated swimming pool. Showers gave me the creeps, I said, and to tell you the truth, I don't even like to drink a glass of water.

Dr. Freeman took copious notes. The story was a fat lie, of course. But now I see it as a lie with meaning. I was telling the dear doctor that I was losing myself, that it was me falling into that dark green water and I didn't know how to save myself. This unit was going to be worse than the drug addicts chanting their Twelve Steps and worse than Anne at Michael Reese screaming about the Cornings coming because I'd seen Dr. Freeman's treatment plan and success meant lip gloss and mascara.

But he took my word about the drowning story and wrote down, *fear of water.*

Every week my staff advisor, Nanette, who had a calming voice, sat on my bed beside me and reviewed a piece of paper outlining my weekly treatment plan. This included: "Pt to spend 15 minutes with a female peer in A.M. and comb and curl hair. To experiment with makeup; to look into mirror 1x day & say something positive; Pt to continue to spend 15 minutes with female peer working on hygiene and appearance in A.M."

In addition Dr. Freeman suggested I learn how to dress more like a girl.

"How am I supposed to do that?"

He suggested I talk to my female friends about what kinds of clothes they wear, and what kinds of clothes boys like.

I signed the treatment plan. I had to. There was a line for my name in the bottom right corner, above Dr. Freeman's scrawl.

DONNA SAW ME as a challenge. My ignorance of makeup was like a secret sin. We wouldn't mention it, we'd correct it. She started by placing her red plastic basket—we each had one, for shower stuff—on the bureau near the mirror. She stored makeup in her basket; she was particular and kept the bottles neat, no smears.

One morning about a week after my conversation with Dr. Freeman, I stood in front of the mirror, not looking at myself. My arms and legs felt light and weird, but heavy, too, as if they might pull me down through the floor.

Carol rested on her stomach on her bed, watching.

Donna tipped the bottle of Beige Glow foundation onto her fingertips. A brown pool. She patted the liquid onto my face. Her fingertips were gentle. I closed my eyes and remembered the grubby fingers of Michelle, my slutty ex–best friend, smearing my cheeks with pink powder blush. My heart pounded so hard it was like wings beating in my ears.

"There," Donna said. "A good start." Coated with Beige Glow, my face looked like tan paste. I looked ill, which seemed appropriate. Donna placed the bottle on the dresser. She picked up a compact of blush. She had real confidence in her supplies. The brush was soft on my cheeks but I don't know, soft or hard, I didn't want to be touched.

Blue eye shadow next, a baby blue with a sparkle in it to bring out my eyes which are like blue marbles. From her bed Carol said, "I wish I had your eyes." Hers were like gray bathwater.

The eyeliner wand was scary-looking, long and thin, like a needle. One slip and you're blind. If James Bond had an eyeliner wand he'd push the end and a dart would fly out.

Donna said, "Don't blink now, keep your eyes closed." Her voice was breathy. Boys on the unit thought she was sexy. She knew it. Her hand was sure, like a feather brushing my eyelid. I saw the blackness on the inside of my lid. I was thinking it was better this way, to let Donna take over my face. Inside, I'd know I was faking. I'd know. And if I lost track—I'd go comatose. Which would be okay because I wouldn't feel anything at all.

"Such thick lashes," she said, "what I would give for them, you don't even need mascara but a little bit might add definition. Open your eyes so I can get the underside."

The rectangle of mirror appeared, but I didn't look. Not looking was key.

Lip gloss in dabs. Whiff of strawberryish scent, but way sweeter. She said, "You should use gloss all day since your lips are on the dry side."

Stepping back, she put her hands on her hips. "What do you think?"

She meant about my face. I sneaked a glance and it was a jolt. My beige face gave me a creepy dead look. The blue eye shadow, the blush—I looked like a stranger. Michelle's friend, Linda—the one who would let boys do anything to her and who could stand to lose about a half a pound of makeup from her face—laughed her mean ha-ha laugh in my ear.

Over the edge, they said at Michael Reese, when Anne started throwing paper cups of juice in the lounge. She's gone over the edge. I knew this edge. I felt it now under my sneakers. You had to walk the edge without looking down, casual-like, so you didn't let them know you were on it even though, like now, your neck felt hot and your legs trembly as if you might sway and tip over. Going over the edge—I'd never done this, exactly. It was tempting. I could feel myself sliding a bit because it wasn't me with the makeup on my face, it was happening to someone else, but it was me, and it would be so relaxing to take the fall, to join the ones who tilted and babbled and threw things. Although, in spite of my violent reputation, I wouldn't be a thrower. I'd be the one in the corner, rocking herself, my arms around my curled-up legs, like my dog Pudgy under the coffee table.

It was nice to have an option, even if you never used it.

I packed myself down smaller and smaller. I had to speak. The hunky counselor George lurked in the hall in his tight rugby shirt, waiting to hear my comments on this newfound beauty. I saw him through the two-inch space where the door was open. For a second I could hear him breathing. No, that was me.

I told myself I didn't care that I looked like a dead stranger. I was good at this—not caring. I had perfected this state of mind. It hid a multitude of fears. My grandmother would tell me have faith, you're on a path, God is watching, but what path could I be on when I looked like a dead stranger and I had a mother who didn't want me as a daughter, a father who put me in the lunatic asylum, Frank the hit man who placed his enormous thing in my hand and me stealing the Dinty Moore from the store?

Say the words. Make George happy. The words don't mean anything. Do it for the points. Without the points I'd never get the sun on my face in the courtyard and a moment outside alone to remember myself.

My voice was flat. I was an accomplished liar, but these were some of the hardest ones I ever told.

"I love my eyeliner."

"I like my blue eye shadow."

My feet moved into the hall. I was unreal. George said, "You look really nice today, Daphne."

"Thank you."

Back at the sink in my room, I washed off the whole gobby mess.

MY NEW SELF was pleasing. New self: girly-girl dead stranger.

From her closet, Donna offered me one of her blouses, the white one with buttons down the front, a round collar and shoulder pads. My first time with padding. One pad slid around and gave me a hunchback.

With the blouse I wore my new jeans, the ones with no rips. Same old sneakers, the Adidas with the creases in the white leather, but neat enough.

Dr. Freeman was pleased. He sat back in his chair. When he shifted his weight, the seat cushion wheezed. "Progress," he said. I tried to smile. The muscles in my cheeks resisted.

All the people I'd never pleased, if they could see me now. Mrs. Langley in home ec with the flushed spot on her cheek, a souvenir of my palm. My mother behind her locked door yelling, *I hate you, go away.* I would please them with my pleasing self. My self begging please, please, stop, my father snapping his brown belt, Frank with his hand on my head, pushing me down to his gleaming zipper.

Dr. Freeman said, "Keep up the good work." He seemed to really like me. I walked out on strange legs.

It had been noted that I sought out female staff members to talk to, not males. A problem. I was encouraged to talk to males of any variety, staff or patient. I complied: *Pt observed interacting w. males more often on shift.*

We had goals. Goals=points. We had morning goals: showering, shampooing, putting on makeup (a special goal for me), cleaning our room, going to school—which was a classroom down the hall, the same row of cubicles I'd sat in when I'd been in rehab. Afternoon goals had to do with school, group therapy, crafts and acting out feelings, verbal or nonverbal. Night goals: going to bed on time. In between were other point-collecting schemes—giving a staff member a backrub, for instance, or doing a good deed, which meant helping another patient, like acting out Nick's screaming mother so he could collect points for role playing.

I was a point fiend. Stuck in the back pocket of my new jeans was a folded-up point sheet; I carried it everywhere, in case an opportunity arose. I had twice as many points as anyone else on the unit, maybe three times. It felt good to be accumulating something—it was like stacking the cans of soda at Michael Reese or watching the numbers flip up on Asteroids. There is a comfort in having a lot of something when everyone says you have nothing, you are nothing. I'd already reached Level 2 and was on my way to Level 3. The staff considered my enthusiasm excessive: *Seems to be focusing on quantity rather than quality.*

One afternoon I had to act out a nonverbal. In the lounge—a small area, a couple of couches, blank walls, deliberately nonstimulating—I asked one of the attendants if I could act out a feeling for him. His name was Brendan, a neatly dressed, jeans-and-sport-shirt, condescending-but-friendly guy. He asked, "Could I choose the feeling?" He was this way—trying to play therapist. I said yes. He said "caring" and asked me for a hug.

I didn't want to hug him, okay? But I couldn't think of how to get out of it. He could write me down as "uncooperative" and subtract points. If I didn't have enough points to walk a hundred feet to the school classroom by myself, an attendant would have to come pick me up.

Up close Brendan smelled of Polo cologne, powdery, as if he'd just taken a shower. Polo was popular on the unit, a couple of the attendants wore it. A nice clean scent, but still. Who was this guy? I didn't look at him.

He said, "You're so rigid." As if I should have flung my arms around him. As if.

I said that getting close to people scared me.

Brendan flagged down George, another attendant. "Hey, give Daphne a hug, will you?" George came at me, arms open, rugby shirt, big pecs and Polo wafting from his neck. Backing away, I said I didn't like to hug, it scared me to get close, people always left one way or another.

Brendan said fine, and wrote down five points on my sheet, which pissed me off. "Why only five?" I asked. He told me that if I gave a male a real hug he'd give me more points.

George stood in his penny loafers; he had all the time in the world. I did it. Never mind the roaring in my brain, the noise like being under the 'L' tracks when the train rushes overhead.

Brendan said, That's great, and crossed out five and put in ten points.

ONE THING about Town House: I don't remember any windows. The unit was at the end of the hospital in a maze of corridors. Some of the patients' rooms must have had windows on one side, but I don't remember them. From the inside I couldn't see my goal—the two lawn chairs in the courtyard, the place that would be my place, the sun that would shine in my face, alone.

I had to remember the courtyard from when I'd looked out the window in rehab. I did remember. I wouldn't forget *out*.

THREE, four weeks passed. Every morning Donna put on my makeup while Carol lay on the other bed, watching. I stood before the mirror and closed my eyes and sometimes I was outside in a field playing on the girls' softball team of Schaumburg, Illinois. I was rounding the bases, legs pumping, on my way to home plate even though I was standing still. Donna and Carol thought I was in the room but I wasn't.

Donna brushed my hair and sometimes she heated up the curling iron so the front part would feather back. My staff advisor said, Why don't you experiment with nail polish, for fun? This was one of my treatment goals: to learn how to have fun. I thought fun would be lifting weights if the hospital had a gym tucked away someplace. I didn't mention this. When Donna painted my fingernails, I chose clear and shiny. I wouldn't let her do frosted pink.

I was walking around the room, shaking my hands so my nails would dry, and Donna said, What about the way you walk? My walk was like this: A bit of bounce, a slight roll from heel-to-toe. A strong walk, with my weight in my feet. Even though the rest of me was locked up inside this place, I was an athlete in my footsteps. I didn't move my hips. I didn't have hips, to speak of. Not like Donna's hips, rounded curves that made a shelf for her to rest her hands on. Donna wanted me to walk skittery like a bird. Like the pigeons in the park near my mother's apartment, strutting, with their chests sticking out, their tail feathers wagging.

She said, Try this. She came up behind me and placed her hands on my hips. Sweet about it. She knew I was in deep about the femininity stuff, she was trying to help, so I tried, too. I took a step with my right foot. She moved my hips to the right. Left foot, left swing of my hips. Step, swing, step.

I thought, *Forget this.*

With my new face on, compliments swirled around me—in the lounge, in the classroom. *You look nice today, Daphne.*

Donna had a skirt hanging in her closet, but she never wore it; a skirt wasn't cool on the unit. I never mentioned skirts or dresses, although I knew Dr. Freeman was hoping I would. That game I didn't even try to play. Dresses led to stockings and fancy shoes and teetering down the hall like an idiot.

At night in our beds one of us would start giggling, probably me, I was always an instigator. I'd moved to the lower bunk—I'd told Carol I was afraid of heights, a fat lie. Now I'd try to lift her mattress with my feet. We'd get giggling and the attendant would open the door and say, It's after eleven o'clock, what's going on in here?

I'd say, I'm glad you came in. I'm trying to go to sleep and Carol and Donna are really getting on my nerves.

As soon as the attendant closed the door we'd crack up laughing again.

FOR ONE of my goals, I had to walk around with my black binder and ask my peers to say positive things about me. I still have the list:

> *you're understanding and smart*
> *you're cool*
> *you don't cut people down*
> *you have good taste in music*
> *you take people serious*
> *lovable and have nice eyes*

MY HOSPITAL PHYSICAL turned up a problem with my thyroid. A hot nodule, whatever that meant. I thought, Great. When Dr. Freeman said, Now about this identity problem you discussed with Dr. Abdullah, I said, What if this thyroid thing is cancer?

I said, I have to take a test, they're going to inject blue dye into me, I'm terrified of needles, will my skin turn blue, I'm afraid of going into the tube of that machine.

He was a kind man, Dr. Freeman. He nodded with concern. Somberly, we discussed my feelings about illness and death.

It wasn't cancer. I had to have a thyroid operation, but that wouldn't happen until my next hospital.

I COULDN'T STAY at Forest Hospital, which specialized in short-term treatment. The doctors said I needed long-term. The transfer to the Wilson Center in Minnesota was going to happen, was not going to happen. Would be happening next week. Three weeks. Was under evaluation. My father was freaking. If a spot opened at the Wilson Center, I'd have to go for four days of interviews to see if they'd accept me. Over the phone my father told me, "This is really important. You've got to get into Wilson, do you understand?" He was like a deranged parent trying to get his kid into the best prep school. I'd have to wow them with my mental illness.

Dr. Freeman said, If you don't go to Wilson, we'll keep you here for three years.

Three years. Donna and Carol and everyone else in Town House—they stayed at most six months. I'd be the oldest living patient on the unit, like Anne at Michael Reese, the screaming one with the split personalities, the legend, the one who was there forever.

The makeup deal—the only reason I could do it was I knew it was short-term. Three years—I'd fall apart.

THE STAFF took me off points. *Obsessive-compulsive behavior,* they said. I could collect only signatures. I collected them. I hit Level 4 in early June. They couldn't deny me. I was going outside, alone.

To prepare, I washed off all my makeup, lather, rinse, lather, rinse. Wore my ratty tee shirt, torn jeans, sneaks. Someone loaned me a watch so I could keep track of every minute I was outside.

Having the outside privilege was a humongous deal for me, but in front of Donna and Carol, I didn't make a big thing out of it. Maybe it didn't mean as much to them. They knew they were getting out in a couple of months whereas I had to inhale every free breath available.

Thirty minutes I had from sign out to sign in. Through the metal door, past the school rooms, through rehab, through the lounge of Country House, turn right. Dead end by the elevator. Wrong way. When I'd gone outside for p.e. class, I'd been following someone else. I traced my steps back, hurrying. Turned left after Country House. I saw the revolving door, stepped in, spun, out. Warm air on my face, blue blue sky, sunshine throwing shadows off the building.

The courtyard was a few steps away. Now that I was in it, I could tell it was a crummy patch of grass surrounded by the red brick walls of the building, but I didn't mind. The two chairs were white, wooden with slatted backs, positioned next to a table with an umbrella stuck in the middle. One side of the courtyard had a view; it opened onto a dinky parking lot. Across the lot was a school playground surrounded by a chain-link fence.

I lit my first Benson & Hedges Menthol, the smoke of choice in mental institutions, I don't know why. Also the smoke of choice in prisons. Later, on the outside, when I'd light up a Benson & Hedges Menthol someone might say, Oh, you must have been in prison.

At the school, it was recess. I'd seen the school when my father and I drove into the hospital, but I'd never seen kids out playing. Grade school kids ran around, tagging each other, screaming and laughing. I sat back. The wooden chair was comfy, the back slanted

at a good angle. I blew the smoke toward the sky. The air was a soft-
ness on my bare arms. No one was watching me. Nine months of
surveillance: I'd survived seclusion, I'd hugged the males, I'd walked
around with gobs of blue on my eyelids, and now here I was.

Two kids chased a round rubber ball into a corner. The ball
shot out in the other direction and a herd of kids ran after it. I
couldn't take my eyes off the kids, their flashing legs running, running.

All I could see was the school and the leafy green trees around
it. But I knew from the drive in that beyond the school were a couple of industrial buildings, deserted-looking. I was at Forest Hospital in Des Plaines, Illinois. I didn't know where the street went
from here, how to get from this street to any other place. I didn't really know where I was.

I smoked the cigarette down to the filter, lit another one off it.
I figured I had time enough for two smokes, plus the walk back. The
kids were running like wild. Their legs were short; they must have
been seven or eight years old.

I stubbed out the cigarette at the last moment. When I stepped
into the revolving door I could still hear the kids screaming. Laughing, I guess.

I'D HAD IT with the femininity discussions. I'd rather be a drug addict than walk around with this crap on my face. I told Dr. Freeman,
"I really am an alcoholic. Yeah, and a drug addict. I realize that
now." There weren't any authentic addicts on the unit, so I wouldn't
be insulting anyone with my lies.

6/9/82 Daphne talked today about the fact that she in-
deed had been abusing more drugs than she had admitted
after coming into the hospital, she states that in spite
of that she feels that she has much better control of
herself. We also talked about her feelings that her parents want her to stay sick, so they have somebody to take

care of. She is quite pleased with the transfer to the Wilson Center, which will take place on Monday morning, June 14th.

—, M.D.

I wanted the staff to know I could take care of myself. I couldn't say, *I'm independent, I don't need you,* so I got into stories.

6/9/82 Pt stated to teacher that upon leaving she was going to have to buy her plane ticket to go to Minn. I asked how she would get that much money. Pt stated she had $250,000 of her own from singing & films she had done. Pt also said she had $50,000 from an uncle who had died. I told her that was a lot of money.

—, Teacher

Saying good-bye, I cried. The tears started as a tightness in my throat, a burning in my nose, water filling my eyes until it dribbled down my face.

I walked around with my black binder and a pen and had everyone sign my journal. It was my yearbook.

Dr. Abdullah wrote: *Ms. (Daphne) Scholinski, I was sorry to see you leave M.H.—after all we did enjoy all those intellectual defenses they taught you at Reese! Well, it's worked out well & I'm sure the Wilson Center is going to help you tremendously. All the best. Dr. A.*

One of the nurses wrote: *Try being a little girl more and an old lady less.*

Donna scrawled in her round penmanship: *When you first came here you were really closed up . . . I'm really glad we got to break the ice before it was too late . . . Look for me in the movies. I really love you a lot and I'm going to miss not having you around and I'm going to make sure someday we're going to meet again. Love ya.*

The young boys on the unit were the sweetest. I'd been their buddy, their coach. One of them, Barry, a big guy, wrote: *To: Daphen I hope you make it wherever you are goning. Because you are a sweet cheek . . . But*

I hope I get to see you when I get out and I hope you don't forget me when you leave here. Do you hear me? I know my witreing is bad but you try to read it untial you get it.

A sad boy named Kennedy, about twelve years old, wrote: *To one of the nicest people I know . . . I felt so much affection for you only God knows how much. I did like you so much now all I can do is hope that I will see you again. Sometimes I want to kiss you so bad and sometimes I want to hit you but all in all I still love you and as I write this I want to kiss you more than ever before.*

THIRTEEN

AFTER WE'D BEEN *living with my father for almost two years, my mother drove to Roselle to pick Jean and me up, her first trip to the old house since she'd gone away to find herself. She was going to drive us to her apartment instead of us taking the train the way we always did. By the front door sat the pots of her geraniums, just brown stalks. Opening the door, she curled her lip at the smell*

which we had gotten used to. She asked, "Why is it so dark in here?" Since she'd left, we hadn't raised the blinds in the living room.

If she wondered what we'd been eating she could see the remains on top of the tv and on the counter by the toaster and on the stove, crusts of green moldy bread and Kentucky Fried bones. "What in God's name?" she said, opening the fridge. She peeked into the vegetable bin where the lettuce had turned liquid and brown. Reaching under the sink she pulled out green heavy-duty leaf bags and got to work, shoving in everything she could find, crusty dishtowels and dried-out sponges and pizza boxes. She filled fourteen, fifteen bags and put them on the curb. "Now go on into your rooms and pack. You're coming to live with me," she said. And we did. We took Charcoal, too.

My mother had moved to Chase Street, half a block from the lake, which was a step up for all concerned but especially for me because Frank didn't know where the new place was. I'd still run into him if I visited my friends on Farwell Street but I liked that I was a mystery person now, I lived somewhere else, and I wouldn't go over to Frank's unless he got me at a weak moment of hunger or loneliness which I tried never to let happen.

Walking home to my mother's through the park behind her building, I passed a couple on a blanket. The guy said, "How are you doin'?" I stopped to chat with them. I was fourteen and I liked to talk to people; mostly the only person I talked to was Jean and she was ten and leading a protected life under my supervision so there were many things I couldn't tell her. This married couple wasn't old but not young either and the man asked if I'd like a beer and I said okay.

"Cigarette?" the woman said. She had a Swedish accent and ultra blond hair. I said I had my own and lit up a Marlboro. Would I like to go to their apartment and have dinner? The man and the woman smiled at me in a nice way; every time the woman spoke her accent was soothing. At their apartment they played Pink Floyd on the stereo, which made me feel at home. They invited me again and I ran down the back steps from my mother's through the passageway between the buildings, up a flight of stairs to their back screen door. The second time I was over the man kept his hand on my shoulder a long time. His wife started rubbing my back and my mind emptied out and I was a shell being rubbed. The wife spoke in a quiet voice and said she and her husband liked my body because it was so boyish. Their hands went further and further and my mouth couldn't speak any words. I felt the husband's beard and mustache touching my skin, a soft feeling. When I left their place I walked around not knowing where I was and without knowing why I went back again a few days later. I could lie on their bed and feel nothing while they touched me. Nothing. Until I couldn't take it anymore. When I saw them in the park, I walked the long way around the block to the front of my mother's apartment building.

ON SHERIDAN STREET an old, wrinkly guy lived in a divey storefront. It used to be a store but he lived in it now, all full of junk and garbage. He wore baggy clothes with his butt hanging out. Super dirty guy. I walked by one day and he said, "Hello," and I said, "How are you doing?" and we got to be friends. I was the only one who looked in on him. From the corner store, I stole Chesterfields for him, put them in my pockets. He introduced me to his neighbor, who was into gold. So from the drugstore I stole religious necklaces with crosses and brought them to his neighbor's house. He gave me Placidyls, sleeping capsules that made me feel drunk.

At my mother's I stole marijuana from the tin beside her bed. I'd slip some into a baggie. She'd go hysterical when she found out. I didn't even want it. I gave it away.

In the city I worked at whatever jobs I could find because I knew I had to make my own money. My mother was always broke and I'd tell her, Don't buy me food. Jean's best friend's mother ran a diner and hired me as a cook. Eggs, bacon, toast, I got good at it. I stole from the diner, too, five dollars here, five there. The woman who hired me knew. She watched me at the cash register. After a while she didn't want me to work there anymore.

All the money I stole, except for a little bit, I gave to my mother. I guess she figured I'd earned it.

Another place I worked was a gas station kitty-cornered from my mother's backyard. A guy named Matt ran the station—he had one regular arm and one stubby arm that stopped at the elbow, where he had a finger and a thumb. The station was self-serve and he'd let me pump gas for tips, if an older person didn't want to get out of the car. I'd stock the shelves and he'd give me a microwaved cheeseburger, an orange soda and a pack of Marlboros, which seemed to me fair pay. He let me sit with him behind the counter. A customer came in, a business guy in a suit, and Matt handed him the change between his thumb and forefinger. We watched the business guy's hand hesitate before reaching for the money. After the guy left, Matt chuckled and said, "I felt like saying boo to that guy."

He must have been born with his arm like that. I thought he was strong to carry on the way he did, unfazed. If he could run a gas station with a thumb and a forefinger there was hope for a misfit like me, too.

At my mother's, Jean and I lived in the finished bedroom in the basement. She played with Snoopy and I turned up the volume on "If You Want Blood" by AC/DC. One time my mother came down the stairs like a horse and screamed at me to turn down the music. Jean was somewhere else that day. I put my face up close to my mother's. She backed off, scared, and picked up the red phone receiver. I wouldn't let up. I yelled at her. She swung and struck my arm with the phone. A surprise. This was the only time she ever hit me. She hit me and hit me and hit me. I stood up and grabbed a rowing oar I'd stolen from the park district; I kept it leaning against the wall. I held the oar and thought a long moment but I couldn't hit her with it.

I ran out of the house with my mother screaming behind me. My friend's mother was a nurse and she thought my arm was broken. It felt like it was going to fall off my body which would have been a relief.

I stayed out until everyone was asleep. Sneaking in, I took the car keys from the hall table. I'd never driven. Inside the car, the green vinyl seat was frozen stiff from the winter cold. I turned the key and the engine roared up. Slipping the gear into reverse, I took my foot off the brake, and the car jumped and the movement scared me so much, I turned off the engine. I sat in the dark, my breath making puffs of steam. I'd have to figure out some other means to get away.

FOURTEEN

THE MINNESOTA ROADS were flat, flat.
They made me nervous, going on and on
like that, you couldn't see the end, you just
kept driving and out of the tunnels of
green corn something eventually emerged,
a faded silo or a huge-headed cow looking
you dead in the eye.

We were driving back from the movies

in Owatonna, a speck of a town; I'd been at the Wilson Center for almost a year. This was before the trouble. It was a hot spring night and we had the windows rolled down from the sticky heat. Everybody's hair blew all over the place. You could hardly think with the wind and the roar of the Wilson Center station wagon, which was a diesel and louder than God. I didn't mind a few moments alone with my mind blanked out although it wasn't going to last.

I sat up front next to Pam, the student volunteer. I liked being up front. I pretended I was staff. In the backseat, Denise said, "Cut it out" to Toby, who was pulling on the tips of his fingers, soothing himself. I swiveled around to give Denise a look and Toby stared at his lap and snuck a pull on his fingertips, just a bit, he couldn't help himself. Denise sat with her legs pressed together so she wouldn't touch Toby's leg; she could be snotty this way. Next to her, Andy peered at his super-neat writing in his notebook and to no one in particular he said, "Guess which Beatles single was the first to enter the charts at Number One."

Denise turned to the boys in the way back, the seat that faced out the rear window. "Did you hear something?" she said.

Craig said, "I don't think I heard anything."

Andy rocked in his seat, his upper body swayed back and forth. He repeated, "Guess which Beatles single was the first to enter the charts at Number One."

From the way back, George said, "I definitely didn't hear anything."

We rounded a curve. I glanced to my left and saw a lake—a swirl of blue, some yellow mixed in, a rash of magenta. It looked like a lake. I thought, I don't remember there being a lake. Is my brain cracking? Where is the other side of the highway? The lake was enormous. Have I gone around the bend entirely? How could I never have noticed the lake? I almost said, Hey, look at the lake over there, but I didn't.

From below the horizon the sun was shooting color into the clouds. No lake, only clouds and sky that looked like water.

Beauty had been around me, there was no end of dazzle green in the Minnesota trees and the fresh-mowed grass; at night, the stars hung like a jillion knifepoints. But mostly it felt as if beauty had nothing to do with me. Now I stared at the purply red and the streaks of yellow and swirly blue and the beauty slipped inside me; I kept my face turned to the window so no one would see the feeling rising in my throat. I think it was joy.

Andy said, "The first Beatles single to enter the chart—"

"Shut up, Andy," Denise said.

"Nyet yet nyaaaa," said Andy, a Three Stooges man. He snapped his fingers, hit his right palm with his left fist, snapped, hit his right palm with his left fist, snapped, slapped the back of his hands right, left, right, left against his knees.

Into the rearview mirror Pam said, "Knock it off, all of you," and I gave her a look of sympathy. *They're so immature.*

We took the Faribault exit and Pam flicked on the headlights. Turn right, then left after the truck stop, past The Curve—the bar that served 3.2 beer and wrinkly hot dogs—and over the train tracks. Past the sewer plant which stunk like every rotting, decaying, farting thing in the universe. "Pew, man, roll up your windows," yelled Craig from the way back, which was my seat of preference if I didn't get the front. You could put your feet up and look into the air at all the places you were leaving behind.

Mosquitoes flew at us, drunk on the sewer, they must have had no sense of smell. We rolled up the windows. Up the hill, turn left into the Wilson Center, the home for wayward adolescents with mental disturbances. The campus was all leafy with brick buildings that looked like a boarding school, or so the staff was always telling us. *We're like a boarding school with lots of therapy,* they'd say. It gave us something to tell the world that sounded a lot better than *psychiatric hospital.* There were about fifty of us patients and tons of staff. By the time we parked the car by Old Main, it was night.

Toby headed off to his dorm. He had trouble with doorways. We watched him as he walked toward the heavy metal door, turned to the right, bowed so he almost hit his head against the doorjamb but not quite, stepped back, forward, bowed again, stepped back, forward, bowed, back, forward, walked through.

"Jeez," said Denise.

As often as I could, I signed up to go to the movies in Owatonna. I kept hoping the sky on 35W would look the same way, magenta with streaky yellow and blue. I wanted to see the colors again, to know they were real, I wanted the beauty to wash over me. I was sixteen and I wanted to find joy but the sky was always different.

INSTEAD OF SKY COLORS, I watched movies—hours and hours in the dark falling into someone else's life: *First Blood, Star Wars, Cheech and Chong: Still Smokin', Breathless, Harold and Maude.* When it wasn't movies it was bowling, or go-carting, or a trip to the Battle Royale all-star wrestling match that had the boys on the unit worked up into a lather; one boy pushed his way to the front of the arena and caught one of Hulk Hogan's sweat rags.

Out and around we were regular people except for the attendants at our elbows—although they were young college students or locals with high-school diplomas, not superior types like the psychiatrists. It was no hardship unless you thought about what you didn't have, such as a family who wanted you at home. Better not to think about that. The staff wrote: *Daphne's mood seems good.*

Up the concrete steps to Unit A. My room was the first on the left, next to the stairwell. In the beginning I was the only girl on Unit A, the first girl ever, eleven guys and me. All the other units were co-ed, a mix of psychotics, violent types and regular depressed people, so there was no reason to throw me in the all-male unit, they could have shifted a depressed boy around. I suppose they thought throwing me to the boys would encourage my girly-girl side. I thought, Okay, I can deal with this, I've always been friends with boys. Then three or four of them wanted me and some of them were strange, they'd been locked up for mysterious reasons that had to do with violence and maybe a girl and God knows what. The second day I was there one of the Unit A boys told another boy to stay away from me, I was taken. I didn't even know who these boys were.

The creepiest one was Sven. He was large and clutzy, looming in my doorway. He loomed, he knew he loomed, he liked that his looming scared people.

I didn't invite him in. I held my pet guinea pig on my lap; I don't know why the staff let me have a pet, but they did. His name was Charlie, he was black-and-white, long-haired, built solid with big buck teeth.

Sven asked me if I wanted to have dinner with him in the cafeteria. I said no, thanks.

Cocky, menacing, he said, "You don't know what you're missing." His fingers on my door frame were huge.

I heard that after Sven left the Center he wound up in court on conspiracy to kill his parents.

The boys walked into my room. Just walked in. A little guy named Clint who loved to drink Amaretto sat on my bed and played video games on my tv. He shot at the aliens flying around the screen; the aliens killed him and the game ended. I played one game until I got killed, then Clint played another. Clint lingered. I wandered out to the lounge and came back and he was still sitting on my bed.

Liam wasn't from Unit A, but he liked to visit from Unit H. He told everyone I was his girlfriend. He wore denim overalls and sat on the floor of my room, a look of absolute devastation on his face. He thumbed through my albums looking for mopey music—the Carpenters. He couldn't find anything mopey enough. He was at least eighteen, heavyset, one of the oldest patients, ready to settle down. I sat on the edge of the bed, chewing my fingernail.

He said, "Someday we'll move to the mountains," and I said, "Liam, I really don't want to do that. I don't like the mountains. There are snakes there." He said, "When we're married we'll move to the mountains, have lots of kids and we won't ever have to be around people," and I said, "Let's just be friends."

Doug was a small-boned guy who played the drums. I put on a David Bowie album for him and he flipped. He asked me to the Valentine's dance in the cafeteria and we had our picture taken in front of red construction-paper hearts; he was my sort-of boyfriend. I think I kissed him a couple of times. We lasted maybe two months.

Liam complained to the staff that he couldn't get anywhere with me. I talked to the student volunteer about the situation. She wrote in my chart: *Daphne expressed that a more serious relationship would slow down her treatment here.* Later, another staff added: *said to have gotten the relationship more under control and she needed room to breathe.*

All this male heat—it seemed to have nothing to do with me in particular.

When Denise arrived—she could have them. She had sex a bunch of times, although I don't know about an actual boyfriend. She took grief about being chunky. Also, her glasses were thick; magnified, her brown eyes seemed as if they almost crossed. But she tried to look nice. She wore makeup, which I'd given up since Forest Hospital, and pretty clothes, which I'd also abandoned. This staff didn't care how I looked, not yet anyway.

I don't know why Denise was at the Center. Her family was messed up, her father was in jail because he fell through the roof of a store he was attempting to rob.

Some of the boys kept after me, but most of them looked elsewhere. We settled into our true bond as exiles, teenage fugitives trapped in a mental hospital.

WE EACH HAD a number. Someone would say, mad, "You're nothing but a number." Then later, the same thing, only as a joke. "What are you, a number or something?" When we went bowling we put our numbers on the electronic scoreboard instead of our names, goofing around. My number was Constance Bultman Wilson (CBW) 682. Denise would say, "Hey, 682, you're up."

    1 pint Amaretto for Clint
    1 pint Jack Daniel's for Drew
    2 pints Bacardi 151 for Doug and me
    2 pints peppermint schnapps for Denise and Fred

At first Fred wanted beer but Doug and I told him no, beer weighed a ton and was hard to hide and besides if you get caught drinking you might as well be drunk and hard liquor would be faster.

Doug and I took the orders because we were making the liquor run. We met in his room, played "Run Like Hell" by Pink Floyd super-loud, got pumped. I slipped off to the gym, shot a few hoops with a patient. We played PSYCH, our version of HORSE, where every time you missed a basket you got a letter until the word was spelled out and you lost.

The unit staff called the gym and the attendant said, "Yeah, Daphne's here," and I knew I'd been checked. Doug heard the staff check on me, sauntered by the front desk and made sure the staff saw him, check.

It was 8:30, already dark. We met behind the chapel and dropped down through the trees, hanging on trunk-to-trunk because of the steepness of the hill, running fast like Rambo through the jungle, jumping over fallen branches, skidding around. Fifteen minutes to get to the road into town, panting. A car drove by and we rolled into a ditch for the James Bond thrill of it. Doug was so small he could hide in a gutter. In town, which was about five blocks long, we walked regular. The off-duty staff could be anywhere.

The liquor store stood like a beacon, brightly lit, so we hung around the parking lot waiting to find someone to buy for us. It wasn't hard. In Minnesota, it seemed as if you were either in rehab or an alcoholic; it was that kind of state. A guy drove up, about nineteen. We gave him the money and the orders and hoped he'd deliver. He did. Twenty minutes to run back, since we were going uphill and carrying a load. We stashed the bottles in the woods, then back on the unit for checks, la, la, la.

Doug and I snuck out and retrieved the goods. I stuck one bottle under my arm inside my jacket, stuck a couple in the waistband of my pants with my shirt hanging over them. Delivery time. At Clint's door, I sauntered in, "Hey, how are you doing," then pulled out the Amaretto.

A couple of us met in Evan's room because he had the best speakers, giant ones with the covers off so you could see the woofers. He was a rich kid from New York with a Mafia accent. He whipped out his bong from the hiding place in his closet. The bong had been a collaborative construction project. Start with an empty bottle of Pert shampoo, rinse it, leave a little water in the bottom, poke two holes in the sides. Take an empty Bic pen and poke it into one of the holes.

Connect the end of the pen to a metal cap from the cable tv hookup—after a while, hardly anyone had cable tv; all the hookups were on bongs or had been captured on confiscated bongs. From a baggie, pinch a hunk of pot that had been purchased from a patient with off-campus privileges. Pack the pot into the cable tv cap. Light up.

Background music was key: the Scorpions or maybe the Doors begging us to come on, light my fire. Volume had to be piercing.

We sat in a row on the edge of Evan's bed, our feet on the floor. Evan took a hit, it was his bong, he had first dibs. He handed the bong to Doug, who took a hit and handed it to me. Pot was not my specialty but whatever. The smoke filled my lungs. Two hits and my mouth moved funny when I talked; my tongue was a thick dry thing I couldn't manage. I passed the bong to Clint, who took a hit and passed it to Denise, who loved to get stoned and eat Doritos, licking nacho cheese powder from her fingers.

In between we swigged from whichever pint was going around. Following the pints came a tube of Crest toothpaste. I squeezed a dab onto my finger, put it on my tongue and swished it in my spit, swallowed. My breath would hide the evidence.

An attendant knocked on the door and we pretended we couldn't hear him so he waited for the lull between songs and knocked again. In his Mafia voice Evan said, "What dja want?" We turned down the music but we didn't get caught with the pot, although some patients had. We burned a ton of incense. Some of the attendants didn't care or they were clueless or without a sense of smell in their heads. But some were zealots and after a while burning incense was forbidden. We started smoking clove cigarettes then.

I got caught one night at 9:30 p.m., after a party in my room. The room search report listed:

1 partially burnt incense stick
1 empty qt bottle peppermint schnapps
1 bottle Windsor Whisky filled w. ginger ale
various bottles "unused" meds

I lost privileges for a while, but I got them back. All this was baby stuff. The legend was the keg party.

In the back of the football field was a cornfield and in the middle of the field was a pit. Pete got an idea. He walked into town and stood outside the liquor store, waiting for someone to buy him a keg of Bud. Someone did. Pete called for a cab, then lifted the keg into the backseat and got in front next to the cabbie.

"Where to?" the cabbie asked.

"Just start driving."

Pete had the cabbie circle around the Wilson Center to the other side of the cornfield. He rolled out the keg. Another patient met him there. They dragged the keg into the pit.

After dinner, patients started sneaking out to the cornfield. You'd walk and walk, then fall off the horizon into the pit. About forty patients filled the pit. The pit got crowded.

Someone built a bonfire. The joy of it—to be drunk in a pit that the staff didn't know existed. Then people started throwing up; some of the patients were fifteen and had never been drunk. We began crawling out in groups of three.

Rolls of toilet paper appeared; someone had planned ahead. We walked into Faribault and toilet-papered one of the staff houses, draping sheets of baby blue over the shrubs. The police arrived, followed by the Center cars. The officer said, "All right, kids, get in." In a procession, we rolled up to the front door of the Center. What could the staff do? We outnumbered them. There weren't enough staff to put everyone on one-to-one restrictions.

We didn't mind losing our privileges. We'd made nuthouse history.

A LOT OF STAFF liked me. This surprised everyone, especially my parents, and even me, although I'd had hints of it. Even the teachers who'd hated me for swearing and punching and cutting class at Sullivan High School in Chicago—they'd wanted to give me another chance because I had that likable look. At the Wilson Center, the staff let me do the patient orientation. The new ones came in almost every Tuesday like inmates walking through the gate, their faces pulled down, mouths that hadn't known a smile in years. We'd eat lunch together in the cafeteria. I'd tell them, I've been to other hospitals and believe me, you won't find one that will let you have fun like this one. Some of the new patients' brains weren't wired for standard definitions of fun.

At one lunch, a new girl went into the bathroom, came out naked and folded into a back-bend by the salad bar. I couldn't look, nakedness embarrassed me, but there was a lot of giggling; she'd managed to shock us her first day out and we prided ourselves on being a group not easily shocked. A staff person jumped up and said, "Come on, get up," and the new girl rose calm as could be, not sure what the fuss was about.

Later on I got to be friendly with her. Her name was Lucy. She babbled, but if you listened hard enough her rambly words made sense. The real problem was she'd take a cup of boiling water from the cafeteria and pour it on her bare feet. Her feet were in bandages a lot.

Compared to many patients, I was no problem, so the adolescent care workers let me get away with stuff. One of the ACWs was a cute guy named Eric, very toned. I picked him up and carried him down the stairs, piggy-backed. Denise and I tried to throw him into the sprinkler. He loved it.

This was a warm-up prank. My best prank was on Tom, who was in his forties, a sweetheart. Doug and I conspired. We saved our best for Tom because we liked him so much.

This was after curfew. I snuck into Doug's room, took his Walkman headphones and plugged them into the mike jack in his stereo. This little trick, we'd discovered, turned the headphones into a microphone. With the headphones in hand, I buried myself in Doug's closet, burrowing under his dirty socks, underwear, sweaty shirts from liquor runs—totally gross, but worth it.

After checks, Tom walked the unit, looking for me. He poked his head into Doug's room and Doug, fake-groggy, looked up from his pillow and said he hadn't seen me. Tom closed the door. I spoke into the microphone. "Tom. Oh, Tom."

He opened the door again, looked around. Went out.

"Tom. Oh, Tom."

He opened the door and asked Doug, "Did you hear that?"

"Hear what?"

"Someone calling my name."

"Tom. Oh, Tom."

Tom looked in the closet but he didn't see me, which was an indication of the amount of clothing I was under.

"Are you okay, Tom?" Doug asked. "Should I call someone? Are you sure?"

We thought we were a riot.

The student volunteers were perky. A new batch arrived every six months. They were nineteen or twenty years old, college psychology majors, living the normal lives that had fallen out of our grasp. Most of them stayed in a house about a mile away from the Center; their job was to drive us to movies, accompany us to McDonald's and listen to our complicated stories about our families.

My favorite was Karla, who had long bushy brown hair. She was cheerful but not obnoxious. She just didn't think everything was so dire. She liked us, that was it. A lot of the doctors—you could tell they didn't like us. They didn't even know us. They talked clinical. None of our parents liked us, hardly anybody liked us, that's how we'd ended up here, so Karla was a shock. She taped notes on my door: "Hey Scholinski, how's your day going?"

One night she was in my room, hanging out. I was telling her about my mother, my father, my sister Jean and my cat Charcoal, who had been lost for two days, her hefty kitty self wedged between two buildings. Karla said, "That's too bad."

She started rubbing my back. Everybody rubbed everybody else's back; it was typical. Napping was also typical among the patients. Everybody was always falling asleep in everybody else's rooms; we were a tired group.

As she rubbed, she said, "God, you could be any one of my friends. What are you doing here? You're so sane. Normal."

She kept rubbing, as if it were a casual remark. She was talking about me, right then. Not what I could be if I applied myself and learned to dress better and took a few femininity hints. It had been a long time since anyone had said anything that nice about me, maybe third grade with Miss Martin. I was normal. This hadn't occurred to me. I said, "Yeah, whatever," but her words got inside me.

They changed me. I couldn't quite believe what she said—that I was normal—but it was enough for me that she believed it.

Karla's internship was up, she was going back to Reed College in Portland. I hugged her good-bye and started to cry which was so rare for me it made her happy. *You're having feelings, Scholinski.* So she was smiling and I was crying. After she left, I recorded a letter to her on my cassette player—we were allowed to record certain things at the Wilson Center—and walked around the unit. The other patients said, "Hi, Karla," into the microphone.

At the end of the tape I said, "I love you." At the Center, everyone threw around the love word. If Denise was bummed out, for instance, I'd say, Jeez, that's too bad but you know that I love you. When I was bummed out, she'd say the same to me. It got to be annoying, as if I couldn't be bummed out because Denise and Doug and anyone walking by would say they loved me, as if that erased my other feelings. But with Karla it was for real; I knew when she said I love you she meant it, it didn't sound dumb. She gave me a photograph from the day the two of us had gone into Faribault to goof around. I was hanging from a streetlight, my shirt sliding up from my jeans, my belly button showing. She wrote on the back: *This is to help you remember (just in case you forget) that once in a while you and I had some pretty wonderful times together.*

I WAS DRINKING a glass of orange juice in the lounge one morning when Claire on Unit B shrieked down the hall that I'd stolen her bones. She would have shrieked at anyone; I happened to be within eyesight. She couldn't come onto Unit A, she didn't have privileges to leave her unit, so she shouted down the corridor about her bones, her bones.

Bev, the ACW on duty, was no help. She laughed. She was a local kid; this was her career job, babysitting us; debating with a psychotic was out of her league. The amazing thing about Bev was that one day she didn't come to work. The staff said, Bev had a baby. Nobody knew she was pregnant, including Bev. She wasn't even superheavy. Her boyfriend was an adolescent care worker on Unit B; if we had the door open between the units, they smiled at each other when they thought we weren't looking. Some of the psychotics chewed on Bev's invisible pregnancy for a long time. What do you mean she didn't know she was pregnant? Does that mean I could be pregnant?

Clair said she wanted me to come over to Unit B so she could beat my ass which I had coming to me because of stealing her bones. I shouted back, "Give me a break. I did not steal your bones." She persisted. I thought, I cannot believe I have to argue about stealing someone's bones. This is lunacy. I have arrived. I put down my glass of orange juice and walked up to where Claire stood on the edge of the doorway boundary between Unit A and Unit B. I said, "I'm really sorry, Claire. I thought they were mine. I put them back in your room." She turned and walked away, satisfied.

We all got used to Claire's tics. The patients who tried to kill themselves—they were the ones who got sent away. One afternoon after group therapy Tanya climbed up the fire escape to the roof of Old Main. Her hair was choppy, it kept flying in her eyes while she debated—jump or not jump. A couple of the staff leaned out the top-floor window to talk to her; their soothing voices floated above our heads. We stood in a crowd in the courtyard. One of the patients yelled, "Go ahead, jump. Go on, do it. Jump. Jump."

The staff tried to hush him up but we thought he had the right approach. We knew how we were: If you told us to do something, we lost interest.

Tanya got sent to United Hospital in the Twin Cities where there was a lockup unit, seclusion, and patients who were worse off than we were; I pictured the hospital exactly, a Minneapolis version of Michael Reese. A couple of days of that and Tanya stopped talking suicide. She came back.

The depressives were defeated. You could tell who they were by the dreary music coming out of their rooms—"Comfortably Numb" by Pink Floyd played over and over again. I was one of them, even though I mostly played violent music.

The psychotics made life interesting. Peter's mind was jammed—facts, dates, state capitals, wars won, treaties signed. We had science class together along with two other patients. All the classes were like this—tiny. The teacher stood at the blackboard explaining how a seed became a plant. Behind us rested a cart of plants under a fluorescent grow light. The teacher sketched a chalk diagram with arrows pointing from seed to sunlight to plant. Gracefully, swiftly, Peter reached back and popped out the fluorescent tube, scooched his feet up onto his chair, climbed onto the table and swung the tube through the air. He chanted, "Light saber! Light saber!"

We leaned back in our seats. The teacher said, "Peter, come on, sit down." Peter cut the air with the fluorescent tube. "The force, Luke," he said. "Use the force."

Star Wars had made a big impact on us.

The psychotics were okay one at a time, but in group therapy—forget it. My group met in the Unit A lounge four times a week. We had two leaders, a woman and a man; I felt sorry for them. They were therapists-in-training, eager, and in over their heads. About ten of us were in the group. Pretty quickly, Peter dropped out because he was too psychotic to attend, which was really saying something.

Group was noisy. William said, "My mother wants to have incest with me," and then he stood up from his seat, sat down, started to stand up, started to stand up, stood up, sat down. The therapists nodded. Martha laughed. She had trouble being appropriate. A book sat open in her lap but she wasn't reading; she was crocheting. She crocheted like a fiend. On the other side of the room, Philip tried to involve Billy in a private conversation. William tried to say a few more things about his mother but was shouted down by smelly Walter, who said, "My Prolixin is making me crazy. I'm on too much Prolixin. If I weren't on Prolixin I wouldn't act this way. With Prolixin I can't be responsible for my actions."

Billy said, "Shut up about the Prolixin, Walter. It's not the Prolixin, it's you. Your problem is B.O. Got that? B.O."

Billy was at the Wilson Center under court order, I don't know why. He held hands with his girlfriend, Charlene, who said, "I'm stupid, my parents don't love me, I'm ashamed of myself," and then stared off, transfixed. After a few seconds the woman therapist said, "Charlene? Are you with us?"

Tiffany stood up and exited the lounge.

Ted was mature. He wanted to talk about family problems. He said, "No one takes this group seriously."

Jacob had a face that looked like someone had smashed it—kind of stunned and pushed in. He said, "I like getting high. I do. I really like it."

With jerky, hostile gestures, Martha unraveled everything she'd crocheted.

I sat in a corner of the couch with my eyes half-closed, faking sleep. Group scared me to death. — no help

WALTER WAS the only one ever asked to leave group. His B.O. got him out. He wouldn't shower.

Every now and then, a couple of guys on the unit kidnapped Walter. From my doorway I watched them carry him down the hall, holding him by his arms and legs, heading for the shower. It was funny, and not. Walter kicked and swore, he was livid; he always fought back, no matter how much the doctors upped his Prolixin. The boys bullied him into the group shower and I heard the spray of water hit the tile. Sven said, "Try some soap, Walter."

At the front desk, Jerry, the ACW, read his book. Walter's screams echoed off the walls so after a while Jerry roused himself and walked into the shower. "Okay now, let's break it up. Leave him alone." He always waited until Walter had been soaked and soaped before he broke it up.

We all teased Walter the most, maybe because he reacted so violently. We pinched our throats so our vocal cords vibrated, then we said his name, "Wallttterrr." This drove him crazy.

One night Drew was running around saying, "Wallttterrr" and Walter was chasing him. Drew ducked into my room, where I was drawing a guitar spaceship from a Boston album cover. Drew closed the door behind him and barricaded it with my dresser. Walter pounded on the door. Drew said, "Wallttterr." The door shook from Walter's fists. Walter punched as if he wanted to kill. It was scary. I thought, I don't want to be part of this torment.

The next day I invited Walter to my room. First I lit vanilla incense. When Walter came in, I kept the incense burning, one stick hanging from a crack between the door frame and the wall, another in my incense holder, a third in an empty can of Mountain Dew. His smell got buried; vanilla's powerful that way. I showed him my latest drawings—angry faces that were blue and purple with a shot of red. He said, "Cool," which I appreciated since my art therapist said why don't I paint something soothing from nature?

Walter never tried anything with me. He didn't come across as sexual; the drugs left him too spacey. It was no problem to be alone with him, even if he smelled.

THIS IS HOW it started. We had a meeting—the chief psychiatrist, his assistant, the family liaison and me. My therapist wasn't there, although she was supposed to be. I liked my therapist. Her name was Jeanette, she had intelligent eyes and the sympathetic therapist head-tipping-nodding technique that went like this: "Uh-huh." Head tip to the left. "Tell me more." Head nod.

Afterward I wondered why she never found any of my treatment odd, why she didn't stick up for me.

We met in the assistant's office at the end of the hall on Unit A. The assistant—a young woman with poufy blond hair, a dress and conservative pumps—had an office with air conditioning, never mind that the patients down the hall sweltered.

When Dr. Madison was in the assistant's office, he sat at her desk. He was a round-faced nerdy guy who wore old suits. I barely ever spoke to him.

The room seemed dark. I'd spent a lot of time in rooms with people talking about me; they usually didn't call you into a little room to say nice things. I guess they figured that if I was a mental patient my feelings had vanished along with my faculties. They started in about how much progress I'd made in increased attendance at school and participation in recreational activities, a lot of gibberish.

I looked out the window at the football field where two patients tossed a ball around on the grass. We didn't have a football team. Who would we play? If we had a team maybe we'd have class rings, which we all wanted. Silver rings with big birthstones and the year stamped on the side. — *wanted a normal life*

Heads turned toward me and Dr. Madison asked me about my relationships with boys and I had to think fast and figure out what answer they wanted to hear.

"I've gone out with boys," I said.

"Have you ever been sexually attracted to a boy?"

"Sure," I said.

"Are you sexually active with any boy now?"

"No."

He said *preadolescent fixation* and I watched the giant mower sweep over the grass with the maintenance guy sitting in the seat up front, circling closer and closer to the two guys and the football.

Even if I didn't understand everything Dr. Madison said I got the drift. He was starting in on the gender thing again. I don't know what got him going. Maybe it was because I didn't want to date the crazy boys. Maybe he didn't like the looks of me.

He could keep me here. This was what I believed. He didn't have to say it for me to believe it was true. He could keep me here because I liked Rambo and didn't go to the nurse to ask for birth control, like Denise did. He'd keep me until my time ran out and I was no longer an adolescent, I was an adult mental patient. Into the state hospital for me.

Walking out of the meeting, I had that girly-girl dead feeling again.

After dinner I called my therapist. First I had to convince the ACW to let me make the call, then the switchboard put the call through.

Jeanette had missed the meeting with Dr. Madison but I didn't tell her about it. I just wanted to hear her voice. She said, "What's going on?" and I said, "I've had a hard day." I couldn't explain. After a while she said, "Don't worry. We'll talk about it tomorrow."

A week after my phone call to Jeanette, I sat on a cushy chair in the lounge for a haircut. Phil, one of the adolescent care workers, cut everybody's hair. He didn't have any training, he just liked to do it.

He put a sheet on the floor and a towel around my neck. His silver scissors snipped around my head. I said, "Leave the top a little longer." My idea was to grow my hair so it covered my eyes. I could hide behind my bangs.

"Whatever you want," he said.

Morris, one of the staff, walked by. Phil said, "Pretty haircut, huh?"

"That's affirmative," Morris said. He was a huge *Star Trek* fan.

Psychiatric Supervision and Medical Management
Daphne Scholinski
3/31/83

. . . We also discussed the problems the patient has with her gender identity but the patient has not really been able to become more expressive in the area of her sexuality and feelings. She dresses like a boy and is often mistaken for one when out in public, although more recently she has had her hair styled and cut in a much more feminine appearance. We feel that there is considerable identification with the aggressiveness of males and the patient is competitive with her father for the affection of her mother. . . .

I wanted to go to college and study art. I was not overly encouraged. Art was a fine hobby but my lead teacher suggested I have a practical skill. The only thing I could think of was to become a probation officer—I thought I could help kids like me, I'd know their bullshit. To be a probation officer I'd have to study police science, learn how to use a gun. That had an appeal.

I told my lead teacher, "I want to be a police officer."

She said, "Oh."

I could see it was not exactly what she had in mind.

In the end, it didn't matter. I didn't know that having been a mental patient would make me less than desirable for police work. No one told me this. No one told Cliff, either—he spent all of his time in his room with kits building models of the space shuttle. He wanted to be an astronaut. The first ex–mental patient in space.


```
Treatment Plan Review
Scholinski, Daphne
4/13/83


    . . . It is felt at this time that an Identity Disor-
der should be ruled in as an additional Axis I diagno-
sis. This is manifested by Daphne's problems with
defining long term goals and career choice, friendship
patterns, sexual orientation behavior, and also some
difficulties with group loyalties. This does impair her
social functioning and has been evident since her admis-
sion . . . The goal related to this identity disorder is
for Daphne to come to terms with herself as a sexual fe-
male human being. The objectives by which we hope to
achieve this is for Daphne, as she becomes more comfort-
able, is for her to explore her feelings about herself
sexually and otherwise, as well as her feelings about the
opposite sex, with her primary therapist. We feel that
Daphne has already begun to work on this and this is ev-
ident by her relating to various members of her treat-
ment team more and when she has been referred to by
strangers as a "boy," it is followed by the reaction of
a nervous giggle. . . .




Master Treatment Plan
Daphne Scholinski
4/13/83 Objectives


    Explore in therapy her feelings related to her sexu-
ality and feelings about opposite sex at least once per
week. . . .
```

153

Jeanette closed the door and sat down, a spiral notebook on her lap. I sat up in bed in my tee shirt and sweat pants, smoking my first cigarette of the day, 8:15 a.m.

Therapy was in my room four times a week; she came to me, I didn't have to go to her. The first fifteen minutes were free association. I said, "Hello." Jeanette wrote this down. I said, "You're sitting on my laundry," which got Jeanette to smile, although she wasn't supposed to react or speak until the fifteen minutes were up. She removed a couple of clean, folded tee shirts from the chair and put them on my desk.

I told her some kids were going to see *Mad Max* tonight but I didn't know anything about it, I should ask my mother, who's a filmmaker, you know.

Silence.

"Do you like David Bowie?"

I got up and put on "Changes." We listened.

"Do you want a sip of apple juice?"

No answer.

"I wonder if Charlie likes apple juice. Charlie could use some therapy. He's running around like a madman in his cage."

Another cigarette. "Sometimes I wish I had someone to take care of me like I take care of that guinea pig."

Scribble, scribble. "I'll slow down so you can have a sip of your coffee."

She wrote that down.

"I've got a question. How come when I ask anyone why I'm here, they can't answer. Don't you know why I'm here?"

Her head bent over her notebook.

"How much longer do I have?"

She took notes on everything. For a couple days, goofing around, I wore sunglasses and a necktie knotted loose around my neck. I looked like one of the Blues Brothers. I took a picture of myself in the mirror to document my coolness.

Jeanette wrote in my record: *Daphne has worn a tie several times this month, once when her former therapist was visiting campus. We are attempting to explore more her masculine dress but she is not very willing or comfortable with this.*

Nothing spontaneous came out of my mouth. Everything I said went through a filter in my brain.

```
Treatment Plan Review
Scholinski, Daphne
6/8/83
```

Axis I: . . . Daphne continues to show the following symptoms related to her identity disorder: problems with her sexual identification, friendship patterns, and in defining long term goals and career choices. These impair her social and occupational functioning and subjects her to distress; Daphne still attempts to mask this by stating she does not care. The two major goals of treatment at this time are for Daphne to eliminate her depression and to come to terms with herself as a sexual female. . . . Daphne has not begun working on the objective of exploring in therapy her feelings related to her sexuality and her feelings about the opposite sex at least once per week. This objective still remains. . . .

I said to Denise, "I have to get out." We were sitting on the floor in her room. She wrote down directions to the house her mother and stepfather owned in Springfield, about a hundred miles west of Faribault. Her stepfather and her mother weren't there. They were living in Palm Springs. Denise said their Springfield house was the biggest house in town; it had an indoor pool. Everyone at the Center was always bragging about their rich families. I wanted to see this house.

It was June, a mild evening. I had a light jacket on, sneakers, jeans, tee shirt, a little bit of money in my right front pocket, the rest of the bills stuck down my sock. After dinner I passed behind the chapel and moved down the hill through the trees as if I were on a liquor run. It felt good to be outside in the air, getting out of this place. My plan was vague. After a stop at Denise's house, I'd hitchhike to California, where it was warm. I'd lie on the beach under waving palm trees. In my travels along the highways, kindly gas station attendants would give me a bit of work in exchange for cash or a microwaved cheeseburger. While I pumped gas I could ask the drivers about a ride west.

Near the bottom of the hill I heard a crackle and turned around. Through the trees I saw Rochelle and Cindy—friends of Denise. Annoying, giggly girls. I was almost seventeen by then. They were maybe fifteen and acted younger.

I yelled, "What are you doing?"

Rochelle, the short, pudgy one with long dark hair, said, "We're coming with you."

"No, you're not," I said. "Go back."

"You can't stop us," Cindy said. She was taller than Rochelle and her skin looked like she always had a tan. Boys fell for her. "We're going on our own AWOL."

"You can't go on your own AWOL on my AWOL."

"We're coming," Rochelle said.

I walked ahead of them, seething with every step. When cars drove by we ducked into ditches but it wasn't any fun, it wasn't like horsing around with Doug, it wasn't James Bond. We passed the sewer plant and the truck stop and slipped under the underpass of the highway. When we got on the edge of Highway 60, a two-lane country highway, I stuck out my thumb; Rochelle and Cindy hung back on the side of the road.

Two farm boys in a white Impala picked us up. The three of us got in the back, Rochelle and Cindy giggling their heads off. The boy in the passenger seat said, "Do you want to get high?" Rochelle and Cindy said yeah. I shook my head, no, and leaned against the side window, my arms folded against my chest. They passed around a joint. Great. Now I was traveling with two stoned dip-heads.

The boy who was driving, he had on a jean jacket, he said, "You guys are from the Wilson Center, aren't you?"

"No, we're not," I said. "What makes you say that?"

"I can tell," he said in a know-it-all voice.

"Well, we're not," I said.

The farm boys took us as far as Mankato. Rochelle said, "I've never been this far from the Center," and I shot her a look.

"I knew you were from there," the driver said.

Rochelle said she was starving so we went into a Waffle House at a truck stop. Rochelle and Cindy hung over the jukebox and put in a quarter for a be-boppy song, swung their hips around, drew attention to themselves when all I wanted to do was skate through. At the table they dragged their french fries through the ketchup. Super irritating.

We got another ride on Highway 14 and then we walked for a long time. Rochelle said, "My feet are killing me," and Cindy said, "Can't we stop?"

I said, "No. If you don't want to walk, stay here."

They stood. "See ya," I said. They followed me. We got another ride through New Ulm and Sleepy Eye. Then we walked some more.

At five in the morning we arrived at the doorstep of Denise's house. It was fancy-schmantzy. Cactus in the front yard, gravelly stones instead of grass; very Southwestern for a house in Minnesota. We looked inside the windows. Yup, a pool.

We didn't have a key or anything. We weren't planning on staying there. I had to figure out what to do next.

I sat on the front steps and smoked a cigarette: that had been my initial goal, to have a smoke in front of Denise's house. Sitting on the grass, Rochelle took off her sneakers and socks, moaning, and Cindy started giggling about how funny Rochelle's toes looked, one of them was really long, and I thought, I've had it. I cannot go on with these two slugs. My only hope was to ditch them and set off for California by myself. I took a drag on my cigarette, considering the image of myself walking alone down the highway. The image unnerved me—what if weirdos picked me up? Rochelle wiggled her toes in the air. She was so young and immature. Cindy was no better. How could I leave them? It was impossible. As the mature one, I had to take responsibility. I stubbed out my cigarette on the stoop.

I said, "We're turning ourselves in."

This was okay by Rochelle and Cindy.

Near town, we saw a light in a warehouse and heard the sound of machines running. I walked in the door with the two of them lagging behind me. I stood for a couple of minutes before a guy looked up from his machine and said, "Can I help you?"

I wanted a quick response. "I'm an escaped mental patient," I said. "Please call the police."

The guy stepped back. One of his buddies got on the phone, pronto.

A sheriff and a deputy arrived with messy hair and puffy eyes; we'd gotten them out of bed. The town was so tiny it didn't have a place to hold us so they drove us in a squad car to New Ulm. We sat scrunched up on the floor of a locked waiting cell until we heard the Wilson Center diesel station wagon arrive.

Four staff were stuffed inside the car: a driver, plus one staff for each of us, like a posse bringing us in.

My privileges were stripped. I told my therapist Jeanette, the ACWs, everybody I could find, the same story: "I wanted to go AWOL to see if I still liked running away. I discovered that I don't so that's why I turned myself in."

Jeanette said, "It sounds like the experience was valuable for you, Daphne, and you have profited from it." She said that after a brief period my privileges would be restored.

In the lounge two telephones sat on a desk. One was interhospital. Patients could answer that phone, if they were near. When it rang, I picked up the receiver. "Cell Block A," I said.

WE COULDN'T BELIEVE IT. We heard the FBI was here. We piled out into the courtyard. A couple of dark blue cars were parked next to the dorm. Unmarked cars. We recognized them from *Hill Street Blues*. I pressed my nose against the window of one and cupped my hands around my eyes. The interior was immaculate. Further proof of the FBI.

We got the story on the tv news that night. There was a camera shot of the Wilson Center driveway. One of the ACWs' cars had stalled out at the end of the driveway earlier in the day. His green

Pinto kept showing up on tv; the reporters weren't allowed on campus. One of our teachers, a man, had been accused of sexually molesting a former patient, a guy named Stuart. A lot of the patients didn't like Stuart, they thought he was a queer. He talked in a high voice and gestured a lot when he spoke. Stuart was a friend of mine; he had a campy wit.

One of the agents wore mirrored sunglasses, just like on tv. A bunch of them disappeared inside the medical records office. They were alone with our files. We weren't allowed outside our unit, because of the news helicopters flying around; we weren't supposed to be on film because of confidentiality, which didn't make sense when there were men downstairs reading our charts. My chart was full of gender stuff. They'd find out there was something wrong with me, something beyond repair. I hid in my room, smoking, worrying they'd take me away someplace.

Patients began to be called in for questioning. After questioning, they weren't supposed to talk about it. At group therapy, people started yelling, "Fuck the FBI. I don't trust anyone. I'm not saying anything anymore." A guy whose record was confiscated wouldn't come to group, he wouldn't leave his room.

We found out later that the officers weren't from the FBI. They were from some state agency. The teacher stopped working at the Center, but we never found out what really happened.

I TOLD JEANETTE an old boyfriend called me on the phone. This wasn't strictly accurate. I'd called him. But he had been my boyfriend, more or less. I met him a couple of months before I went into Michael Reese; he was a house painter and he painted the apartment my father and his girlfriend were living in. He was about thirty. I was fourteen.

I didn't tell Jeanette how old he was and I don't think she ever asked.

His name was Bart—very thin with blond hair, tall. He rode a Harley and I rode on the back of it, my hands on his waist. We rode into Busse Woods, a forest preserve where a group of guys with Harleys and young girlfriends hung out by a picnic table, drinking beer and smoking pot.

At Bart's apartment, we sat on his cushy beige couch, watched tv. I'd meet him after school. Bart wasn't pushy about sex. If I said no, that hurts, he stopped.

I wasn't afraid of him. He was sweet to me. But I never loved him or anything like that.

When I called him on the phone from the Wilson Center, I knew he was in a relationship. So it was just chitchat.

I told Jeanette, "We're talking about getting together after I get out of the hospital. I'm really in love with this guy. No one compares to Bart. No one."

She nodded.

I said, "It's so hard to be apart from him. It's torture until I can see him again. I really think we were meant to be together."

Endless Love was my source of love information.

Treatment Plan Review
Scholinski, Daphne
8/3/83

    Axis I: . . . In the last three weeks Daphne has begun
to explore her feelings related to her sexuality as well
as her feelings about the opposite sex. Up until three
weeks ago she was not discussing this and we wish to continue this objective where some progress is being made
now. . . .

What I left out about my feelings for the opposite sex was huge. I didn't tell the doctors or my therapist and they never asked.

At night I remembered things. I didn't want to go to sleep; I didn't know whose face was going to show up when I closed my eyes. Sometimes it was Frank, leading my hand to his zipper. Whole scenes played themselves out in my mind.

I had this friend Nick in Chicago. We were sort of dating but I don't think we ever kissed. I hung out at his family's apartment and one time I fell asleep on his bed. I was always tired. He had a twin bed with a blue down comforter on top. I slept on top of that. Nick wasn't in the room; I don't know where he was, getting something to eat in the kitchen, maybe.

As I slept, a weight pressed down on my stomach. A body heaved itself on top of me. I started to push even before I woke up. A balding, slimy head pressed close to my face.

"Get off me," I said. I pushed him away. "Get off."

He was disgusting. Nick's father.

Psychiatric Supervision and Medical Management
Scholinski, Daphne
8/10/83

. . . Overall she has shown a definite and positive attachment both to her therapist and to the overall treatment program here.

Her themes in psychotherapy are more related to the here and now with plans to enter college to study art and making some more definite goals for herself in the future. We hear little lately of preoccupation with the past, with distorted stories, and there is little acting out in terms of stealing from peers here in the hospital.

She also has some concerns with her femininity and has formed appropriate male peer relationships although she is not sexually active.

This new guy came and I did his patient orientation. His name was Luke and he was born without a sense of smell so you could fart, throw up, whatever around him and it wouldn't bother him. This was one of the first things we knew about Luke.

He slept with a friend of mine, Sally, for a while. He was cute, with dark hair that curled up on the ends when it grew a little long.

Lots of people were sleeping around; sometimes the staff would give lectures about how this was hurting our treatment, mostly nobody cared. Sally, Luke and I hung out together, listening to music in each other's rooms. Sometimes we all crashed for a nap in Sally's room. Then he and Sally split up and he asked me out and I said no. I didn't think of him that way.

At the gym we played pool: Denise, Peter—who knew the names of pool champions—Luke, me and a young patient, Eliot. I was trying to keep Eliot occupied. Otherwise he'd be in his room sniffing Liquid Paper. He stole bottles of it from the Center secretaries.

I had my own pool cue which unscrewed into five pieces that fit in a case. Another patient had given it to me—he'd stolen a bunch of pool cues from a cargo train parked in Faribault. My pool cue made me feel professional. The wooden handle was carved and felt good in my hand.

The gym closed at nine o'clock and it was my job to lock up; I stored my pool cue in the workout room. Denise left to get some donuts at snack time, Peter wandered away, Eliot ran off to his room with a guilty look on his face—I could tell he was going to do a little Liquid Paper sniffing before bed. Only Luke and I were left. He was wearing jeans and a green hospital scrub shirt. We all wore scrubs—souvenirs of our time on locked wards. Luke said he wanted to talk. I said, "Okay." We walked over the grass to the right side of the football field and sat down under the second tree.

He leaned forward to kiss me.

I said, "Luke, no."

This baffled him, the word no. A cute guy like him?

The rest of it was as if I was in a camera looking down from the sky.

He forced his hand into my pants. I shoved his chest and tried to move my knees up, but he leaned his weight on my legs to keep me down. At the base of my throat, he pinned me with his left forearm. I heard his breathing getting heavier. By the time he pushed inside me, I was already someplace else in my head.

The girls' shower was down the hall on Unit A; it was like a regular bathroom for one person. That night I took it over. I was in there for about an hour. Someone knocked on the door for checks and I said, "Yeah." I never told anyone. I thought if I told my therapist she'd want to know why exactly didn't you want to sleep with Luke, a fine, handsome boy even if he couldn't tell the difference between a fart and Jean Nate after-bath splash?

A couple of days later Luke approached me in the cafeteria, casual. "How's it going? Do you want to hang out tonight?" I walked away.

A video was playing in the chapel that night: *Badlands,* one of my favorites. The only movies we weren't allowed to watch were *One Flew Over the Cuckoo's Nest* and *The King of Hearts;* the staff thought the films would give us ideas. I preferred a violent flick, anyway. Rick, Denise and I sat together and pulled up a chair to rest our feet on.

In *Badlands* Martin Sheen played Kit, a misfit on a shooting spree. When he killed a man, he had a surprised look on his face, as if he didn't mean to shoot him but he had to, out of a demented sense of self-protection. When threatened, he'd kill. As he pulled the trigger, his eyes went icy. That's how I'd wished I could be, icy and capable of revenge.

FIFTEEN

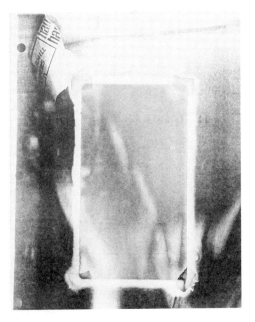

THESE HOUSES STARTED to go up across the street from the Wilson Center. All day the sound of hammering. From the dorm windows we watched carpenters in overalls lug beams around. Who would want to live near us? We didn't like living near ourselves.

The houses turned out to be low income. What do you know.

We climbed into the first house closest to the road; it was partially built and without a roof so the October night came straight in on our heads. The air was cool and fresh; the stink of the sewer had abated. One of the new boys hoisted each of us up to the second floor using his clasped hands as a step. Then he boosted himself but not before passing up a two-liter bottle of orange soda and vodka mixed together so you couldn't tell what you were drinking. After that came two pints of schnapps and a pint of Jack Daniel's for Drew, who wouldn't drink anything else.

Drunk as fish we got, six of us, leaning against each other on the empty floor, passing the bottles and smoking cigarettes, which we flicked out onto the dirt when they'd burned to the stub. I had a moment of relaxation then, I think we all did. I forgot what kind of girl I was or wasn't, I forgot Dr. Madison and his meetings. We liked being together, away from the staff, away from the doctors and their reports, just us; we didn't have to figure out the right thing to say, we could say anything and it would be fine. There was one guy, his name was Ray, he was handsome with soft curly brown hair, but not sweet. After he'd been into the schnapps he stared at me strangely; I knew he thought the devil communicated with him, he got a narrow-eyed look. I turned away but I didn't tell him to stop. We wouldn't do that to each other; we'd heard enough of the word *no*.

One wall of this house was covered with black tar paper and had a window cutout but no glass. Sitting on the floor I stretched my neck up and watched the beam of the flashlight of Francis McMullen, a security guard, move over the lawn of the Wilson Center. "Yoo-hoo, Francis," I called out, but not loud enough for him to hear me. Denise said, "Cut it out, Daphne," and used this as an excuse to nudge Ray in the shoulder; he may have had a strange Satanic look in his eye but he also had handsome soft curls so she was interested.

Francis McMullen was a small man who feared us, which we knew, so we tormented him, although we didn't have to, because he tormented himself. Once when the heater clanged during a staff meeting, he jotted down the duration of each clang on a piece of paper until one of the staff said, "What are you doing, Francis," and he said, "Do you hear that clanging? They're sending messages through the pipes in Morse code. They're going to take over the place."

He was out there now with his beam of light, searching for Rick, Drew and Ray, who had missed their checks and didn't give a rat's ass, or so they said, but after a while we couldn't swallow another drop so we jumped out the side of the house and tumbled onto the ground. Denise became quite giddy and deliberately rolled into a new boy whose name was Hugh; he had the chiseled face and body of Tom Cruise and was rich besides, so he was used to girls throwing themselves at him. Hugh was okay as long as he took the lithium. Perhaps vodka plus lithium was not recommended, but we didn't think that way then.

Everyone scattered and I managed to perch myself on my bicycle. I had been promoted to off-campus housing by then and had more freedom to come and go. The bike wobbled horribly, I could barely hold the handlebars. I pedaled the back roads of Faribault, weaving in and out of the lanes, and when I came to the house where the student volunteers lived I dropped the bike, I could go no farther, even though my house stood two blocks away. My house was called Gull House, though there never had been a gull spotted in Faribault. As soon as the bike fell to the grass, I tripped over the front wheel.

At the door, Owen, who was clueless, said I did not look well and would I like to come in and wait for Dory, who was the student volunteer I'd often visited. She was a friend of Karla's, the one who had rubbed my back and told me I was sane and normal, which I'd never forgotten. I managed to say that would be fine and while climbing the stairs to Dory's room I lay down, so this is where she found me when she came back to the house. She helped me into her room and I threw up in her wastebasket. She determined that things had progressed to the point where I had to be reported. After folding me into her blue Honda, she drove me to the Center and escorted me to the nurses' station where I breathed into a tube and was officially pronounced drunk with an alcohol level of 1.5 percent. Word that I had been caught spread through the dorms quickly.

The Center had a policy of not letting a drunk person go to sleep. I guess it was for safety because people have been known to choke on their own vomit, but I thought the policy was idiotic. The plan was to walk the alcohol out of me. Dory took my arm and I jerked away. I said I could walk by myself and then I swerved so she grabbed my elbow and I relented. As we circled the dorm a few patients hung out their heads and cheered for me, *woo-hoo, Daphne.*

We approached the walkway that connected the main dorm with Unit R. I looked up in my drunkenness and in the light stood a new girl, her name was Valerie, watching me. Even standing still she had a sad manner, which I have always found appealing. I'd met her a few times, I'd done her patient orientation, but I hadn't thought much about her one way or the other. She was small-built, with short, wavy dark hair and an intelligent expression on her face. That night when I looked at her it seemed as if she was looking right into me, seeing me. I felt calm. I knew she would be my friend, I don't know how I knew, it was an odd feeling, but it turned out to be true.

Even after all the trouble, she said she'd known that night that we would be best friends, which a person certainly needs in a mental hospital as well as anywhere else. I had never honestly had a best friend, someone I could speak freely with and who liked me the way I was and who wasn't pushing me to the ground to smudge red lipstick on my mouth. So the prospect of it made me happy, which was a rare feeling for me.

ALL THE WHILE in my two years at the Wilson Center I was making my plans to get out. Making my plans. Other patients I'd known, like Evan with the Mafia accent, had been discharged. I wanted this for myself. Dr. Madison said that if all went according to plan I could leave in August. I wasn't sure what this meant—if all went according to plan.

A lot of discharged patients enrolled in their hometown community college—we did not have grandiose expectations, no one talked about Yale. Some patients stayed in Faribault and worked busing tables at Country Kitchen or pumping gas at the Spur gas station; this was the kind of job we felt suited for. Other patients disappeared into halfway houses close to where their parents lived.

I'd flunked freshman year at Sullivan High School in Chicago—
I'd earned seven-eighths of a credit, not even one whole credit. At
Michael Reese Hospital I couldn't concentrate in class; after I'd been
in and out of seclusion, I couldn't hang on to the point of school.
The same at Forest Hospital, when my face was beige and cakey with
makeup. I was a doomed mental patient so why should I multiply
fractions which I already knew how to do anyway? I'd slipped two
years behind. Now I wanted to get my high-school diploma on
schedule. I didn't want to be twenty years old and just getting out of
high school. I didn't want that. So I studied, which was a novelty. I
asked my teachers if I could do extra credit and they said okay, so
each semester I took double credits. I thought if I had the diploma
it would be one less reason for the doctors to keep me here.

Reading was hard for me. I'd never admitted this. Ever since
grade school when I'd felt bored in class, the words had looked
mixed up on the page. When I wrote a word I flipped the letters
around unless I concentrated hard. I didn't know about dyslexia, I
just thought I'd be blamed for not doing it right.

Also, I had trouble remembering what I read. It didn't stick. I
could remember what the teacher said, but not what I'd read. I never
said anything about this and no one ever noticed. From an early age
they pegged me as a troublemaker and this was as far as their interest went. Now in class, I worked around the reading confusion. I listened to the teacher and read slowly and studied the words I wrote
to make sure the spelling was right.

labeling

Even as I studied, I worried that someone could stop me from
getting out. If the doctors wouldn't let me out, I'd run for it like
Rambo. I'd live on the streets and they'd never find me.

THE DAY AFTER my drinking episode, I visited Valerie on Unit R
since she didn't have privileges to go off-campus to my house. We sat
on Valerie's twin bed in a corner; she leaned against one wall and I
leaned against the other. On the stereo she played a classical record,
violins and piano; she didn't own Pink Floyd. We talked. Every word
that flew between us was of interest—our mothers, the other hos-

pitals we'd been in. She looked at her hands as she talked. She was shy. I liked this. I was shy, too. Hardly anyone knew about my shyness, but we knew it about each other.

I told her things I'd never told anyone, things about my family. I told her I was afraid at home. She nodded. She had a way of listening that invited me to say more. Anything I said was okay by her. Her acceptance—I floated in it. It made my fear recede. All the scary things: Sven looming in my doorway, seclusion at Michael Reese, my father with his belt. All this loneliness seemed survivable, as long as I could tell Valerie about it.

Toby stuck his head into Valerie's room, or tried to. He turned to the right, bowed so he almost hit his head against the doorjamb but not quite, stepped back and Valerie said, "Toby, what is it? What do you want?" He stepped forward, bowed again and she said, "Stop it, stop, Toby." He stepped back, froze. "It's time for dinner," he said.

As soon as he left we giggled like maniacs, we couldn't help it.

THE NEXT DAY Valerie went AWOL with another girl, Fiona, who was a troublemaker with a slutty way of chewing gum; she kept her mouth open, which showed you more than you wanted to see, silver fillings and a pulpy tongue. I didn't know the reason for the AWOL, but I could imagine. Valerie hadn't been at the Wilson Center long and the first weeks were the hardest, before you'd *adjusted*.

Word traveled. I said, "I want to go find them, it's cold out," and one of the adolescent care workers said he'd drive me around Faribault. We took off in the Center wagon, never mind that even if we saw them, they'd have heard us coming and fled. Downtown Faribault was locked up at night except for a few bars which we didn't bother with; the bartenders could spot a patient a mile away. I said slow down and peered through the car window into the alley beside the brick movie theater, but if they were down there in the creepy darkness they were worse off than I knew. We cruised the residential neighborhood, rows of bland Midwestern ranch houses where normal people lived out their lives doing God knows what. I chewed my thumbnail. Valerie was like a small, compact bird. Before she came to the Center she'd studied dance, she was a delicate sort and I felt toward her the way I felt toward my sister, Jean—if I didn't look after her, who would?

The ACW wrote in my chart that I seemed concerned about Valerie. That's what he wrote. Interpretations varied. The next day Chloe, the assistant to the chief psychiatrist, told me I was restricted from Valerie's dorm because of suspicion I had been involved in her AWOL.

We met in Chloe's office, which was beige and tidy, like her. I argued that I had in fact been trying to find Valerie so why would I have been involved in helping her run away?

Chloe said, "You seem to have strong feelings about this." She leaned back in her chair. I was a fly caught on sticky paper.

I disappeared into my room. First thing, I put a Styx album on the stereo. Cranked the volume. My wall was not concrete, like the walls at Michael Reese, but it was hard enough. I banged my fist against the wall with the beat, thrashed my body around, screamed with the music, *No!* Banged, thrashed, screamed *No!* No one heard me.

Banging will only take you so far so I left my room and tracked down my substitute therapist in Old Main; Jeanette was on vacation. I argued with the substitute. Then I argued with the physician's assistant on Valerie's unit. The two of them talked, we talked some more. They agreed to lift the restriction but not without letting me know that it would be hovering over my head and all eyes would be on me, so I'd better watch myself.

Valerie returned with that snake Fiona. I stopped by Valerie's room and picked her up on the way to dinner. In the cafeteria, she piled iceberg lettuce onto a big plate, put a few carrot shavings on top, celery bits, then dribbles of oil and vinegar, mostly vinegar. I knew what was up.

I headed for the vegetarian entree. At first I was vegetarian just to be different. Then I had a wicked dream about having to slaughter a cow, everyone watching me, cheering, the cow looking me in the eye, blood from a nearby dead cow splattering in the air. I couldn't kill the cow. I woke up and that was it. No more meat.

A lot of patients had jobs so I'd persuaded the staff to hire me as a vegetarian cook. Up until then vegetarian entrees were peanut butter and jelly on white; I'd been eating about four a day. Now a patient who was working the line served me up some of my own vegetarian lasagna, nice and cheesy, with broccoli and mushrooms.

We sat with Benny and Rick. Eric joined us, he was the staff member Denise and I had tried to throw into the sprinkler. A staff person usually sat at each square table; family-style, they called it.

Benny had a plate of macaroni and cheese in front of him but he kept looking at Valerie's pile of lettuce, because that's what he'd rather have—he didn't like to eat. He liked to run. Always running. When we played softball, if he wasn't up at bat he'd take a lap around the field, then another lap.

Benny ate the macaroni because he'd lost a bet with Rick. Rick was trying to get Benny to eat. Rick had blond curls, a sweet face, he was an athlete, a football player. He'd challenged Benny to the one-hundred-yard dash. The deal was if Rick won, Benny had to eat.

Benny ate fast. Under the table, his legs jiggled. He wore his usual garb: running shoes, sweats, tee shirt. He ate as much macaroni as he could manage, then stood up.

No one asked where he was going. Where else? He'd carved a groove around the edge of the football field.

A curl of Benny's cheesy macaroni rested on the table near his plate. I flicked it at Valerie. She flicked it back at me. I flicked it at Rick. He had peas on his plate. He lined them up like ammunition and fired them at me. One skidded to the next table and hit Denise. She put a pea on a spoon and ricocheted it over to me.

Eric, the staff member, let this go on. Then he said, "You're being immature." This didn't stop us. We'd been called worse. Peas flew. I liberated a piece of broccoli from my lasagna and flung it. Valerie flicked her carrot shreds. The noise started to rise in the cafeteria. "Okay, cut it out," Eric said. From the far table a patient named Wendell Williams rose, his whole body jerking. "Ahhu, ahhu," he said. His hands pumped the air. He was a sweet guy, but he couldn't stop jerking off. At this point he was displaying considerable restraint. His head flailed around; his glasses were strapped on like goggles.

At the table next to Wendell, Andy started in: "Guess which

Rolling Stones song was the first to hit the charts at Number One."
Beside him, his girlfriend flipped through her notebook. She was a
new patient. A miracle: she was exactly like him. She had a list of
every top-forty song of the past and present.

Eric stood up. "Okay, enough," he said. Wendell Williams said,
"Ahhu, ahhu," as a staff person escorted him out of the cafeteria.

We stubbed our cigarettes out on our plates. Dinner was over.

EVENINGS I SPENT in the lounge on Unit R, Valerie's unit. We'd
have dinner together every night and I'd head back with her to her
unit. I was a wicked backgammon player, unbeatable. I captured her
piece and stuck it on the bar, just like that. She'd have to roll dou-
bles to get out. "How'd you get to be so good?" Valerie asked.

"Lockup," I said. All that Michael Reese backgammon training.

Lucy shuffled up to the backgammon table, her feet wrapped in
gauze with white tape crisscrossed over it. She'd poured boiling
water on her feet again. She held out a drawing for me.

It was a picture of a princess. The princess gown was painted
with pearl nail polish on lined notebook paper. Squished on the side
she'd written: *To Miss Daphne Scholinski, hello hello hello and hello to the most
beautiful, kindhearted chameleon seductress may the warmth from some of Mr. Rod
McKuen poetry gaze its light down on you also the sundown will fall down at your
feet.*

"That's nice, Lucy," I said. "Thank you."

She shuffled off, babbling to herself. I rolled my eyes at Valerie.

I left before curfew. As soon as I got through the door of my
house the phone rang in the kitchen. I ran for it.

Valerie. "Did you get home okay?"

The trick was to talk softly so the ACW in the lounge wouldn't
hear every word.

WE WERE TIRED. Valerie lay down with her head on her pillow. I
curled up on the bottom of the bed. We didn't want to lie on the

carpet—it was gray and rough, industrial. We napped. The late-afternoon sun had already set but we couldn't tell because Valerie liked to keep the shades down. I could sleep like a bandit on Denise's bed, or Rick's bed, or in the car. Sleeping in my own bed at night was harder. I was restless.

An angry voice came into Valerie's room. I don't remember whose voice it was. The voice said, "Get up! Get up!"

A meeting was called. About me. None of the staff would tell me about it. The ACWs I liked—they said it was not their place to tell me.

The ACW from Unit R had called the meeting. I went over to talk to her. She was cool, and pretty; I wanted her to like me.

She said, "We believe you're having a physical relationship with Valerie."

This floored me. I didn't have the tingly feeling with Valerie, the way I'd felt with the girls at the roller-skating rink, the tingly feeling I'd tried to forget about.

"We're not physical," I said.

She looked at me. She was going to win.

"And I don't appreciate people spreading rumors about me," I said. At least I could get in the last word.

The next day my therapist said that after much discussion it had been decided to restrict me from seeing Valerie.

"You are in a paired-off relationship that is not appropriate," Jeanette explained.

I was sitting on a hard-backed chair in her office in Old Main. Since I'd moved off campus she didn't come to my room anymore. If she'd been in my room I would have blasted AC/DC so loud she'd have shimmied off her seat.

"She's my friend," I said. "What's not appropriate?"

"Your friendship is replacing the therapeutic relationship."

I had been friends with Valerie for ten days.

I stomped off. I was a pretty good stomper.

AFTER THREE DAYS, our restriction was lifted, who knows why. We didn't ask those kinds of questions.

Valerie and I squeezed onto the floor of the phone booth, which was a tiny room, the size of two regular phone booths, with a glass window so the staff could see if you were getting upset on the phone. To prove he was mature, Hugh smoked cigars; he'd given us two. Valerie and I lit up. Our goal was to fill the booth with smoke. Puffing away. Puffing puffing giggling.

Smoke rose. We couldn't see out the window anymore. The staff disappeared in the fog. Valerie coughed, then I coughed, okay, enough, we opened the door and smoke poured out. The fire alarm went off in a flash.

The ACW shook her head as we emerged. *Testing limits,* she said.

```
Psychiatric Supervision and Medical Management
Scholinski, Daphne
11/23/83
```

We brought the patient into supervision partly because last night she had wondered if I had heard any of the negative rumors that she might be having a homosexual relationship with a 15 year old female patient who has been admitted relatively recently. We discussed this further today and the patient does not feel that she herself has any homosexual wishes nor past history, and we talked more about her general gender identity and her defining more for herself her direction of associations and actions at this time. She also felt that some of our concerns were that she might be pairing off with a relatively new patient in a therapist-like relationship. We also had concerns that the patient might be pairing off in such a way that she excluded staff working either with the other patient or with this patient.

At any rate, although there may be regressive signs associated with the patient thinking of discharge and future careers for herself, we think that there is no substantial reason to suspect homosexual activity. I see this as a reflection of the patient wanting to be more of a therapist and to identify more with staff at this point and yet not really having the solid training to do

Valerie was flipping out—the conferences about us, the threats.
When she was on the phone, the staff asked her, "Who are you talking to?" She couldn't take it, even though the doctors had picked me
as the instigator. Valerie was the innocent one.

She dug into her stash in the bottom right drawer of her desk:
a box of chocolate donuts, a couple of candy bars, a large bag of orange Doritos chips. I don't know if she ate each item one by one, en-
joying each chocolate donut, or if she crammed in chips and donuts
and Snickers all together. It didn't seem polite to ask.

The food went down fast, then came up again into the toilet. It
was hard on her throat.

She called me. "I binged," she said. We had a moment of silence
for the bingeing.

By the time I got a ride to Unit R and walked down the hall to
her room, she was gone, whereabouts unknown.

A security guy was heading out in a Center station wagon. I
flagged him down and he gave me a lift back to my house. Denise
lived in Gull House now; she'd been moved off campus, too, so I
told her Valerie was AWOL. Just after 1 a.m., I slid up my window
and popped out the screen. The whole house was one level. I hopped
onto the dirt behind the shrubs; Denise followed me out.

I don't know where we thought we'd go. We started walking.
Denise was always good for an adventure.

Five minutes after we left, Valerie showed up at my house. The
ACW, a geek named Simon, said she had to leave. She wouldn't.

Denise and I got tired of tramping around in the dark. We returned to the house. Valerie sat in the living room, her eyes welled
up with tears. We went into my room to talk. She sat on my bed. I
said, What's wrong, and she shook her head. "I don't want to go
back," she said. She started to cry. I thought, We are screwed. She is
sitting on my bed in the middle of the night, crying, and refusing
to leave.

Simon stuck his head in. He adjusted his black glasses. "I've called the residential supervisor," he said.

The Center vehicle rumbled up and Valerie got in. I told Simon, "I hope the Center doesn't take the wrong view about my relationship with Valerie."

ON LITHIUM, Hugh was sweet and handsome, the resident stud who liked pretty girls. In the gym, he lifted weights with good results. The doctors decided to take him off lithium to make sure the drug was working. A med holiday, they called it.

One day he was Hugh, joking around, bouncing a basketball. A few days later he said, "Do you know who I am? I'm Jimmy Page."

We loved Led Zeppelin and we loved Jimmy Page, the lead guitarist. This was interesting. Most patients didn't try to assume the personality of someone who was still alive.

The counselors moved Hugh from his off-campus house to Unit R, for supervision. All day a staff person kept within arm's length to make sure Hugh didn't hurt himself or anyone else. Mostly the staff person sat in the chair by Hugh's desk and watched.

Denise and I went to visit Hugh in his room. He was too busy to really talk. We stood in the doorway. The cover on his stereo had been unscrewed and he held a handful of colored wires. He stood on his bed and tacked the wires in clumps around the wall.

"This is the brain," he said. "Get it? All these colored wires running all over the place. The brain. Wired up. What does the brain need? Let's see. I think the brain needs a smoke. Yup."

He bent down and took a cigarette from the pack on his desk. He stuck it between the wires on the wall above his bed. With a flick of the lighter, he ignited the cigarette. "The brain loves a smoke," he said.

Denise and I descended to the nurses' station in the cafeteria and pounded on the sliding glass window. A tired-faced nurse appeared.

"Hugh's not doing well," I said.

She said they were monitoring him.

"Can't you put him back on his medication?" Denise asked.

She gave us a sympathetic frown. "We don't have the orders," she said.

It always came down to this: the ones who gave orders and the ones who followed them.

A few days later, Rick and I went to see him. Hugh said, "Who are you?"

When the nurse finally came with his lithium pill he refused to take it. "No fucking way," he said. "You're trying to poison me." The nurses kept talking to him, for days, until they convinced him to try the pills, just for a week. At the end of the week, he was Hugh again. His stereo was destroyed but he was back. His med holiday was finished.

Psychiatric Supervision and Medical Management
Scholinski, Daphne
12/21/83

. . . In the psychotherapy process, the patient has clearly formed a therapeutic alliance with the therapist and it may be appropriate at this time to discuss whether or not the patient wants to work on some of her gender identity problems more fully. The patient seems to be fixated at a preadolescent level of sexual development and she might have more themes of homo-eroticism toward the therapist than she feels comfortable in discussing.

We were going out in the world, Denise and I. It was an experiment. A teacher at the Wilson Center had arranged with Faribault Senior High for us to attend two classes. The teacher had arranged for Rick and Hugh to take classes at the private school in town; Rick played football for the school team, got his picture in the *Faribault Daily News*. Denise and I weren't private school material.

We went for an hour and a half a day, to mix with the normals.

There was no such thing as incognito in Faribault. Most of the high-school kids couldn't wait to get out; they knew every person in Faribault and they'd known every person their whole lives. Denise and I pulled up in the Center station wagon. We drew attention walking up the steps. I kept my eyes straight ahead. We sat next to each other in sociology. I don't remember a word of the class. It was so overwhelming just to be there.

My other class was art. It was okay. I had to draw a roll of toilet paper, which seemed dumb.

As soon as our second class finished, we exited. The Center car idled at the curb.

After a while I talked to a few students. They were curious. "You're from the Center?"

One girl was cool. She was the daughter of one of the Center nurses. Her name was Paula. Her ex-boyfriend, Ralph, had a crush on me. He invited me on a hayride. Paula was there, too, a bunch of kids. In the middle of the ride the tractor stopped and I jumped off to pee in the field. I squatted down, felt a sharpness—barbed wire. I'd cut my calf. I was too embarrassed to tell anyone that I'd sat on barbed wire. They'd think I was a mental case. I let the cut clot up and dry.

Peer Review Clinical Conference
Daphne Scholinski
1/10/84

     . . . Identity Disorder Symptomatology: Sex Orienta-
tion. Dr. —— and the therapist discussed this with
Daphne in a supervision. It seems that as Daphne moves
along in therapy she is also experiencing some regres-
sion: By having a best friend relationship with a peer
in the dorm this allows her to regress for awhile. . . .

In February Denise and I flew to Palm Springs to see her mother and stepfather for the weekend. It was called a Therapeutic Leave of

Absence, a TLOA. The doctors thought this was a good idea—
diversify peer relationships. I could go spend the night with Denise because she was pudgy with super thick glasses. Valerie was cute, so one
nap on her bed and forget it.

Denise's stepfather was a rich guy in a silk suit that rippled over
his belly. He picked us up in his big car. He was a car dealer.

"I understand you've got your license, Daphne," he said.

I told him I did. I'd taken driver's ed at the Wilson Center, tooled
through the Center parking lot in a square American car with an instructor. I can't remember if they let all the patients take driver's ed;
it's hard to think of someone like Wendell Williams behind the
wheel, yelling *ahhu, ahhu.*

Twice I took the driving test in downtown Faribault. The first
time, parallel parking did me in. I ran over two orange cones because
I gunned the car in reverse by mistake. "You've just killed two people," said the man from the DMV. "If this had been a real-life situation, they'd be dead."

The second time I took the test, I passed.

Denise's stepfather let me choose any car from the lot. He was
friendly. I chose a beat-up 1979 Nova. He couldn't believe it. He did
a side business in used cars. He said, "Wouldn't you like to try a
BMW? A Mercedes?"

I said, "Nah." The Nova was a sun-faded blue. When you closed
the door the glove compartment fell open. Sitting behind the wheel,
it felt like my car, it felt right.

The next morning we took off on a day trip. The freeways didn't
faze me; all that racing around on go-cart activities paid off. Denise
popped Adam Ant into the tape player. We made a beeline for Bev-
erly Hills.

Our mission was to see *Footloose* starring Kevin Bacon, which was
playing in a fancy mall. We arrived. Denise got a large popcorn, I got
red Twizzlers. We were happy. Kevin Bacon played a rebel, an out-
sider. We loved him for that.

As we walked out of the theater, a clump of young girls in tight
jeans screamed, Kevin Bacon, Kevin Bacon. I turned around. Where?
They looked at me. I had the same spiky short hair he had in *Footloose,* the same jut of the chin. The girls started to move. Denise and

I walked faster and faster down the street, scared, almost running. I thought they'd rip my clothes off. Turn the corner, down a block, then into the Nova. Floor it.

When we got back to the Wilson Center, I didn't say a word about being called Kevin Bacon.

SOMEONE AT THE GYM told me, "Valerie's at the nurses' station."

I took off. I ran super fast across the football field and through the parking lot. I got there in time to watch two ambulance attendants carry her out on a stretcher.

We knew. No one had to say _suicide attempt._

She was allergic to alcohol. After a certain point her pulse would slow down, she'd have trouble breathing. It was scary. She could overdose. We never let her drink that much with us but she'd drink in her room, alone, wicked bummed out.

She never talked to me about how she was going to kill herself. When people are serious, they don't talk about it. We talked about how depressed we were, but that was normal. I tried to keep her going. All the time I told her, "You're a good person, you're wonderful, I love you." I told her that after we got out of the Center, we could travel around together, see the country. I gave her my fortune from a Chinese restaurant in Faribault and she pinned it to the bulletin board in her room: _Courage is your greatest present need._

A little while after this, she went home for a visit. Her parents lived sort-of nearby. While she was home she called me. I liked that I was the one she called. She said she was drunk. She said she'd really done it this time. I panicked. I told her I wanted to tell the staff. She didn't like the idea, but I told the staff anyway. The switchboard operator called the police, who busted in on her.

GIBBERISH FLEW in the air. Dr. Madison leaned toward me, trying to make me understand. "We feel there is a pathological aspect"—he paused, peering at me through his glasses—"to your pairing off with a female patient who has had two suicide attempts."

What response would be appropriate? Nine adults looked at me. We were in a conference room in the basement of the dormitory. The light was poor.

"She's my friend," I said. Who did they think I'd be friends with? Everyone here had tried suicide, or wanted to.

"We feel that your separation process"—more pausing, more peering—"has reactivated some underlying feelings of rejection." He cleared his throat. "You have displaced these conflicts with your therapist and your mother to the female patient."

I had the glassy-eyed look of a moron. I knew about *patholo-gical*. It meant sick. People like Frank, who steered my hand to his zipper. Creepy men. Or creeps like Gloria, the babysitter who lifted up my tee shirt, and Jean's. He was saying I was like them. A sicko.

"In addition," he said, "you have been observed riding your bike back and forth in the street in front of automobiles as if to taunt the drivers."

Evel Knievel bike riding. This I knew about.

"It was fun," I said.

AT NIGHT I STAYED in or went out with townie friends. One night, I came home late. Getting ready for bed, I caught a glimpse of myself in the bathroom mirror. I usually tried not to look in the mirror; I didn't care. I put my face up close to the glass. A couple of dark hairs had grown on my chin. Denise had told me I should get rid of my chin hair and while I was at it, why didn't I do something about that mustache? My mother used to bleach my mustache; she loved doing it, it made her feel like she was taking care of me. I thought it made my mustache look like a white caterpillar on my lip.

I wasn't up to addressing the mustache situation right then. I took my housemate's tweezers and plucked out the chin hairs. With each tug I felt a sting. My chin was smooth.

I was trying.

```
Clinical Management Order Sheet
Daphne Scholinski

    5/7/84 10.00 am Daphne is restricted from contact
with CBW #—.
```

I hurried over to Unit R, turned the corner, headed down the hall. Valerie, escorted by a male attendant, walked toward me. I looked at the pale wall. Included in the restriction was no eye contact. I wanted to look at her brown eyes. I wanted to look. If we looked at each other, we'd send each other a message. We'd know that this wasn't what we wanted to be doing. A look would be a comfort.

I couldn't look at her. Just the wall.

I knocked on the door of Dr. Epstein's office. He regarded me blankly.

"Do you have a few minutes?" My voice was level. I wouldn't let him see my desperation.

"Yes, I do." He was Valerie's psychiatrist, he'd been writing all about me, but he didn't know me by looking at me.

"I'm Daphne."

"Oh." Not a flicker of uneasiness. "Come in."

He slid behind his desk. I sat in a chair, trying not to bite my fingernails. He was distinguished-looking, with white hair and a fancy tan suit.

I told him I didn't understand why the restriction was in place, Valerie was my friend, we weren't physical.

He said, "We think there has been a physical relationship."

We. Who was we?

"No way," I said. "We've never thought about it, we've never discussed it."

He raised his eyebrows doubtfully.

My armpits were sweating. "The idea of being with another woman turns my stomach," I said.

He smirked. "When something turns my stomach, I find that exciting."

I got out of there.

My bike was parked next to the dorms. I took the long way back to Gull House. I pedaled hard. My brain repeated, *I cannot take this one more minute. I cannot take this.* Dusky light made it hard to see. The cars driving downtown had their headlights on. I ducked back and forth in front of them, darting from the right side of the road to the wrong side.

I LOBBED A ROCK at the screen on Valerie's window. She slid the window open.

"Hey, you're going to get in trouble," she said.

"This sucks," I said.

"Yeah. Fuck them."

"Fuck them," I said.

"I miss you," she said. Through the screen, I could barely see her face.

"I miss you, too."

Another night, back at the house, I picked up the phone. The ACW perked up. "Hi, Rick," I said.

The ACW wrote this in my chart, using Rick's patient number: *Daphne talked on the phone with male peer #———.*

"Yeah, I'm Rick," Valerie said. "And you're Doug. Hi, Doug. How's it going?"

Grand Rounds Note
Scholinski, Daphne
5/11/84

She and her female peer have had modifications to their relationship with restrictions to one hour visiting each other daily and one 15 minute phone call daily. Generally, her reaction to this was one of feeling upset about the threat of being separated.

My visit was scheduled for four o'clock, like the arrival of a felon. A nerdy ACW named Emily met me on Unit R and escorted me to Valerie's room. Emily sat herself down. We were not to be left unsupervised.

"Hey," I said.

Valerie and I cracked up, laughing.

"Nice weather, huh?" she said.

"A mosquito bit my big toe."

We laughed some more. Everything seemed hysterical.

TO GET READY for discharge, I moved into an unstaffed house. My room was small and white with a light bulb overhead, like a furnished seclusion room.

We'd been hanging out in my room, Hugh and me, after a bike ride to the park. Hugh went to the bathroom. When he walked back into my room he was like a different person. Cold eyes.

"Hey, what's going on?" I said.

He got his hand into my pants fast, jammed his fingers up me. I was so numb I couldn't move. He grinned at me as if he thought I wanted it.

His hand was so forceful there was blood.

Afterward, I kept trying to figure out if I'd done something to bring this on. We'd never even talked about attraction. Sometimes I wondered if he'd been having an episode, if he'd forgotten to take his pills.

I didn't think anyone would believe that it had happened. A stud like Hugh? With me? I was so full of shame, I couldn't even tell Valerie.

Hugh was in my crowd, though. I couldn't avoid him. When we

were all together, I still had to play Frisbee with him. I still had to smile.

THE REAL WORLD AWAITED. In career-planning class, we wrote our resumes, pieces of paper we'd never willingly show prospective employers. Our resumes were full of jobs we'd held at the Wilson Center, which would lead only to questions we didn't want to answer. I listed: *vegetarian cook, evening gym supervisor, stair-sweeper for housekeeping, medical records photocopier.* Our salary history was modest. The Center paid us a dollar or a dollar-fifty an hour.

The final in the class was a fake interview with one of the administrators at the Wilson Center, an arrogant man who wore nice suits and kept his hair neatly combed. We had to pretend we were applying for a job as an adolescent care worker at the Center. The ACWs had always told me, "You'd make a good staff," so I was kind of interested in the idea.

I made an appointment with his secretary and showed up in my neatest pants and shirt. The secretary ushered me into his office. From behind his desk, he pretended to scan my resume. "So, Daphne, why do you feel you would make a good adolescent care worker at the Wilson Center?" He reeked of condescension.

"I've had a lot of experience in mental hospitals," I said.

Right, like he would ever hire me.

JEAN WAS GRADUATING from Robert Frost Junior High. I flew to Chicago, my mother picked me up and we drove straight to the graduation ceremony, which was held at Conant High School, the school I'd been destined for if my life hadn't taken a curve.

Jean gave me a hug, a bit stiff, then ran off to be with her friends. All the girls wore white dresses with blue and gold ribbons pinned to them like award ribbons. I didn't know her friends. She was taller than a lot of them; she'd grown. She liked makeup, now; she wore foundation, mascara, eyeliner, eye shadow and pinkish lipstick. When had all this happened?

We sat in the bleachers, my mother, her boyfriend, me, my father. I took a picture of my sister's little head in the middle of hundreds of kids. I held the camera up to my face a long time so no one could see my eyes tearing up. She was having a normal graduation. My baby sister, who used to look up to me. She was having a normal life with normal friends. I'd gone to high school with Jesus and Jimi Hendrix and a roommate spazzing out on electric shock which I thought at any minute the doctors were going to try out on me. I'd had a man at the edge of the bathroom stall watching me pee. I'd had points for eyeliner, points for blush, restrictions from my best friend, doctors saying I was a sicko.

I couldn't let anyone see me cry. It was Jean's day.

AFTERWARD we all went to Denny's. I wolfed down French toast. My mother and I were in a rush. We climbed into her boyfriend's black Cadillac Cimarron, a boxy car, and started driving to Minnesota. We drove on the highway through the sunset, all night, and into the sunrise, like bandits. My mother's a night person, like me. We didn't mind the drive. We listened to the music I liked, the music she liked, taking turns. She wouldn't let me drive.

We turned left into the Wilson Center driveway not long before 11 a.m., when my high-school graduation began in the gym. Jean and my father were already there, hanging around outside, looking awkward; they'd flown, but my mother didn't have the money for a plane ticket. The heat was killing everybody.

A mental hospital high-school graduation doesn't attract a lot of dignitaries. It was low-key. Nine patients were graduating in my class. We didn't bother with robes or mortarboards. We got dressed up as best we could. I wore a new pair of silky parachute pants with lots of zippers on them. We sat in chairs on the stage where I'd had dance therapy, which I'd loathed. The instructor had tried to get me to act out my anger toward my father. She'd taunted me to get a reaction, and after a few minutes I'd pushed her and she'd lost her balance. She gave up the idea of me acting out my anger.

Two seats away from me loomed Sven, stuffed into a tan polyester suit.

We each had someone stand up and say a few words about us. My therapist said how motivated I'd been, *exceeding expectations.*

After I got my diploma, which was a fake since I still had to complete a few credits, I was supposed to say a few words at the podium. I couldn't. Nervousness paralyzed me. From the audience someone said, "Come on, Scholinski, say something."

I said, "You come up here and say something," and sat down.

Afterward a photographer took pictures, but it still didn't feel like a real graduation. No school jackets, no homecoming, no prom, no cap and gown.

I introduced Valerie to my parents. She smiled so sweetly it made me sad. Being best friends with Valerie—it was already receding into the past. We couldn't talk anymore. Our visits were always supervised, so I couldn't tell her the real things.

In all my family pictures, someone's got a cigarette burning—me or my dad.

Grand Round Note
Scholinski, Daphne
6/22/84

She has a new hairdo which looks much more feminine than we have seen for a considerable period of time. She still continues to meet with her female companion on another Unit but has not escalated her contacts with her much more, if any, than when we were limiting their periods of visiting with each other. . . .

There was talk of delaying my discharge. When Dr. Madison told me this, I fell into myself, I got quiet. Walking across the courtyard, my legs were trembly. I was a dead stranger again, my stomach clenching up, my mind flipping. *Three years in the hospitals, my high-school years gone. I have to get out, I have to get out.* Dr. Madison wouldn't let me out if I was still close with Valerie. In my room, I wrote myself a note and slid it into my right front pocket. Whenever I needed strength, like when Dr. Madison gave me the beady eye, I put my fingers on the note: *It all seems like a game. I'm not giving up. I'm going to win. Figure out a good strategy. Use the right moves.*

I played Karla's words in a continuous loop in my brain. *I'm normal. I'm sane.*

Super numb: my optimal state. I looked for opportunities to enhance my numbness. Every year around the Fourth of July, the staff set off fireworks on the grass between the pool and Dr. Wilson's house. The Faribault townies parked outside the Center and sat on the hoods of their cars; they didn't want to get too close. For us patients, it was a mini–drug fest.

One patient got his hands on some acid, so I bought two hits from him, five bucks each, Purple Microdot. My friend Drew bought one hit, a bunch of other patients, too. We all wore super-dark reflecting police-type sunglasses, like the guys wore on *CHiPS,* even though it was night.

I put the tiny squares into my mouth, waited for my mind to dissolve.

Drew and I lay on our backs on the thick grass. A Roman candle shot up, left a smoke ring that rose and rose and faded. We didn't care about the exploding colors. We liked the smoke rings.

Valerie wandered by. She'd been drinking, but wasn't drunk. She wore cut-offs and a tee shirt with a leaping dancer on the front. I said hi. As if I didn't care. As if it didn't cost me anything to ignore her, after we'd made plans to travel the country together, which we never mentioned anymore. After I'd told her all my secrets. She knew about my father and his brown belt, about the way I pretended I was Rambo running through the woods, about how missing my sister made me cry. She was the first one who listened to me who wasn't getting paid to do it, and I thought we were going to be together forever. I was going to take care of her. I was going to make it so she'd always want to be my friend.

I let her walk on past. Her sandals flip-flopped on the grass.

After a while, Drew and I got up and walked over to the edge of the Wilson Center pool. He gave me a shove and I reached out and dragged him into the water with me. Our sunglasses sank to the bottom, so we dove after them. With each kick of our feet, air bubbles shot out. The pool lights made everything sparkle. I waved my hand through the water and the bubble trail shimmered.

I didn't know it then, but after discharge, the numbness would stick. I couldn't lose it. I couldn't find my way back to the me before the numbness. I just couldn't find my way back.

Grand Round Note
Scholinski, Daphne
8/6/84

    . . . She is spending less time with her female companion and we see this as a favorable sign.

My insurance ran out August 5, my eighteenth birthday. My discharge was set for August 10, 1984. Dr. Madison said everything was in remission except my gender thing. It was all planned. I was really leaving.

My mother drove up for my discharge party and Jean flew in for the occasion. I was so glad to see them that I hugged them. My mother handed me a box wrapped in rainbow-striped paper with a curvy red bow on top. We drifted over to the cafeteria. Jean wore a sleeveless pink tee shirt with black silhouetted French poodles on it. She'd turned into quite the little hipster.

At 10 a.m., a skinny-armed kitchen worker in a white apron carried in my cake. We hated these sheet cakes. We got them for birthdays and discharges. With new patients rolling in like mad, every week we had a cake: dry and white.

Jeanette and I stood by the cake together. It felt weird to be up there; I was standing in the Wilson Center cafeteria, but my brain was someplace far away, trying to figure out what was going to happen to me next. I cut the first piece, sliced into the fat pink roses.

Squiggly writing read: "Good luck in the future Daphne." Patients passing through on their way to class snagged a piece. They said they were happy for me, but I could tell they wanted to be the one cutting the cake.

I opened the present from my mother. It was a tripod for the camera she'd given me at graduation. "Thanks, Mom," I said. I really meant it. She could surprise me that way—she could give me a gift that made me think she really knew who I was, after all.

This patient named Norm, he was a real stoner, he took photos with the Wilson Center camera, it was his specialty. I didn't know how to arrange my face. How could I be sad to be leaving this place? But I was.

Norm flicked back his long hair, aimed the camera at Valerie and me. We smiled, kind of in a desperate way, with our arms around each other's shoulders. Valerie had more than a year to go at the Center. I didn't know when I was going to see her again. As soon as Norm put his camera down, I slid my fingernail into my mouth for a good chew. Valerie and I had been friends for ten months. Not long, really. But at seventeen, it was the longest real friendship I'd ever had. "I'll write," she said, and I gave her a feeble look.

Dr. Madison had approved a post-discharge plan for me. The idea was for me to live with my mother and her boyfriend in Oak Park, the first suburb west of Chicago, and attend Triton Junior College. Before I left, I told Dr. Madison I'd changed my mind. My new plan was to buy a beat-up yellow school bus and drive around visiting all the discharged friends I'd made at the Wilson Center. I'd sleep on a mattress on the floor of the bus. I'd drive to California, New York, Florida—an ex–mental patient tour of the states.

He was not pleased.

My mother, Jean and I headed for the Cadillac. In the trunk I stashed my suitcase and duffel bags, my rolled-up drawings, my stereo and my boxes of record albums. Exerting my older sister rights, I claimed the front seat. We drove past the courtyard and down the curvy Wilson Center driveway. I looked behind me and everything was the same. Two patients traipsed across the lawn in baggy pants, looking wicked depressed. I popped in the cassette tape of songs I'd made especially for this moment. My mother let me blast the volume. I sang along to "Free Bird" by Lynyrd Skynyrd, followed by Boston wailing about it being such a long time, it was time to be going and would you remember me after I'm gone?

Once we passed the sewer plant, I hung my head out the window. Hot summer air blew through my hair. What would Dr. Madison say? Head-hanging: girl or boy behavior?

I spooled a roll of black-and-white film into my new camera. We weren't allowed to take pictures at the Center, although I'd snuck some.

I held the camera up to my eye. I wanted to forget everything and I wanted to remember everything. I photographed the fields the trees the silos. We were moving fast. I clicked and clicked. I was disappearing; the hospital remained; the hospitals were all I had. They were what had happened to me. As we passed a farmhouse, I snapped a farmer standing by the front door, picking his teeth.

None of the photographs turned out.

SIXTEEN

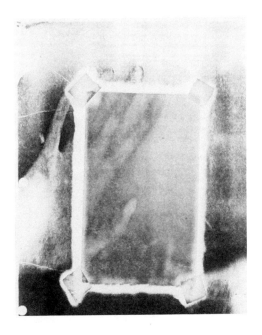

FROM MY BED in San Francisco I can see the sky. I sleep up high, in a loft. I like knowing there's a view out there even when my eyes are closed. Being up high I'm at the same level as my paintings on the walls. I like my art around me but usually not the really disturbing pictures, the ones with the screaming faces from *back then*. I have trouble enough with nightmares, the hospital security guards running after me, their feet pounding. I keep the screaming paintings in my studio.

I have made my own path and more often than not I walk in circles; in the center are the hospitals. I move closer, then step back. I remember little things. A year after my discharge, when I was earning money to go to college, I worked in a factory packing relief food for Africa. My job was to hold a hundred-pound sack while pasty powdery stuff poured down a funnel. Every so often I'd throw in a Tootsie Roll to surprise the person in Africa; I'd think of the kitchen staff at Michael Reese sending me up two Mountain Dews instead of one and what pleasure there is in the unexpected bending of rules.

But I've always been that way, a rule bender.

Dr. Madison would have a bit to chew on if he saw me now with my hair cut short, dressed in shapeless jeans and a tee shirt, *masculine attire* as he would say. When I was in a bar in Santa Monica recently, I stood in line for the women's bathroom. The woman ahead of me turned and said, as if to enlighten an idiot, *This is the line for the women's room.* I've heard this statement a lot. I said, "I know." I looked at her as if she was the fool but inside I was sweating. She reminded me again. I said, "I am a woman." I hated saying that; I have never quite fit in that box. She said, "You don't look like a woman. You don't sound like a woman." What was I supposed to do with that? I was like, "What, do you want to see my i.d.?" I pulled my i.d. out of my wallet, I knew I didn't have to do this but I figured it would end the situation. She took my i.d. and passed it up the line. Each woman looked at my i.d., looked at me, looked at my i.d., looked at each other.

I avoid public bathrooms. I'll never be a girly-girl.

Here's a nugget for Dr. Madison: When I was nineteen I sped down a country road in a 1966 red Ford Galaxie 500, on my way to see the woman who would become my first lover. Thinking of this woman with her green eyes, I felt the tingle in my stomach and I thought, My God, Dr. Madison was right about me. The tingle turned to a retching in my gut. I saw the face of Dr. Epstein, Valerie's doctor, smirking at me in disgust and slimy satisfaction to know that

I had fallen in love with a woman, which he'd long suspected of me.

But I've proven the doctors wrong. I don't feel disgust in myself or in love.

They are the ones who should be ashamed.

I have exceeded expectations, as my therapist would say. I have not killed myself. Benny, who liked to run, he ran in front of a train and died. Eliot, who sniffed Liquid Paper, he got drunk and froze to death in the Minnesota snow. You could see where he'd staggered trying to get back to the Center; on the ground where he fell, his new jeans left smudges of blue dye. The boy who bought Eliot the liquor that night: he was kicked out. When he got home, he shot himself in the head.

I came close, once, after the hospitals. I put the snout of a gun inside my mouth, considered its oily metallic taste. There were circumstances. My girlfriend was cheating on me, the guys at the factory tormented me. I'd been turned down twice for college financial aid because of my father's income, even though his money was no help to me. He said I was on my own, he'd spent a million dollars on me already, he'd paid for my treatment through his insurance plan. I had the long white envelope from the financial aid office in my hand. If the letter didn't say yes, I was going to pull the trigger. I opened the envelope, read the yes, felt stupid.

In college, I selected the thick volume of the *Diagnostic and Statistical Manual of Mental Disorders* from the library shelf. The book rested heavy in my hand. I didn't flip to *zoophilia* the way we had at Michael Reese. I paged through to Gender Identity Disorder. I had to sit down.

From the fourth edition of the DSM, the current edition in use:

Girls with Gender Identity Disorder display intense negative reactions to parental expectations or attempts to have them wear dresses or other feminine attire. Some may refuse to attend school or social events where such clothes may be required. They prefer boys' clothing and short hair, are often misidentified by strangers as boys, and may ask to be called by a boy's name. Their fantasy heroes are most often powerful male figures, such as Batman or Superman. These girls prefer boys as playmates, with whom they share interests in contact sports, rough-

and-tumble play, and traditional boyhood games. They show little interest in dolls or any form of feminine dress up or role-play activity. A girl with this disorder may occasionally refuse to urinate in a sitting position. She may claim that she has or will grow a penis and may not want to grow breasts or to menstruate. She may assert that she will grow up to be a man. Such girls typically reveal marked cross-gender identification in role-play, dreams, and fantasies. . . .

The words are ludicrous, but not if it's you they're talking about, not if it's you they're locking up. Not ludicrous at all for the ones who continue to be diagnosed as mentally ill. A mouthy girl in cowboy boots or a boy who drapes a scarf on his head to pretend his hair is long like a princess—well, they are targets for the Dr. Madisons of the world.

In my artwork, I'm making a series of paintings and drawings from my hospital years. I've sketched the floor plans of every place I've lived, beginning with my parents' house in Roselle, Illinois; there's the room I shared with Jean and the kitchen floor where Pudgy peed. In my mother's apartment in Chicago, I include the basement closet where Joey, my Disciple brother, slept. At Michael Reese, there's the white seclusion room and the bathroom where James and I tried to have sex. On the floor plan of Forest Hospital I sketch the lounge where I sat through all those smoky A.A. meetings.

I draw the Wilson Center landmarks: Walter's smelly room, Evan's room where we inhaled pot from our homemade bong, the football field where Luke raped me. And in the sketch of Unit R, I note the exact location of Valerie's room.

When I am drawing it is as if I am back in those rooms. But the wonder of it is, I'm looking down from above. All that practice in leaving my body has given me an aerial perspective.

Sometimes I wish I could return to the hospital. It's ridiculous, I know. But it's hard to figure out everything on my own. In the hospitals, I lost my ability to trust myself. In any interaction I'm always thinking, I must be the one screwing up.

Also, I know I could have done worse than the hospitals. If my father hadn't had his fat insurance policy, if I hadn't been from a middle-class white family, I could have ended up in jail instead of the psych ward. If I had been a young kid of color no one would have thought I was worth fixing. I know I had to go somewhere; at fourteen I was a wild thing. But I didn't want to be locked up. I wanted be in a place where I felt the way I did when my third-grade teacher told me *sweet dreams* over the phone. I wanted to go where people liked me the way I was. I wanted to matter.

Even though I've made tons of hospital paintings, I can't change what happened. I still wonder why I wasn't treated for my depression, why no one noticed I'd been sexually abused, why the doctors didn't seem to believe that I came from a home with physical violence. Why the thing they cared the most about was whether I acted the part of a feminine young lady. The shame is that the effects of depression, sexual abuse, violence: all treatable. But where I stood on the feminine/masculine scale: unchangeable. It's who I am.

I can't get the time back. We had a Wilson Center reunion on campus a year after I was discharged; about twenty people came, one guy had been a patient ten years ago, now he was a businessman. No one knew what to say. We never had any other reunions.

Every once in a while, curiosity overwhelms me and I try to find people from then. There aren't many I can locate. Denise is divorced and has three kids. She works as a cashier at a Circle K. I like talking to her, but she doesn't laugh the way she used to.

Driving on the highway outside of St. Louis a few years ago, I looked over and saw Cliff in a car beside me—he's the one who built space-shuttle models and wanted to be an astronaut. He waved me down and at the next exit, we pulled to the side of the road. He gave me a big hug. Cliff's wife was pregnant with their second child. He seemed to be doing okay, but he didn't have the glimmer in his eye the way he used to when he talked about going up in the space shuttle. All the patients I know—we're missing that glimmer, the hope about what our futures might be.

My best friend is Rick, the sweet-faced football player from the Wilson Center. He still has his blond curls. We have an understanding. We talk on the phone and I say, I was at a party and everyone talked about their high schools, and he doesn't have to say a word for both of us to know what we've lost—not just a little thing like a senior class ring, either.

Valerie is studying to become a documentary filmmaker. After years of not being close, we've started to talk a bit. When she first found out I liked women, she wouldn't return my phone calls. Valerie—who used to look at me with her brown eyes in a way that said, *Tell me everything.* Losing her—it was unbearable to me.

When I was in college, I'd try to tell people about everything: the makeup lessons, the points for hugging a male staff member, the restriction from seeing Valerie. They'd say, "Oh, really? That's too bad. What are you doing now?"

How could I explain my fits of depression when no one wanted to hear the details? I began to tell my last big lie.

I had a best friend from the Wilson Center, a dancer, her name was Peri. She was the first person I'd ever loved. We'd never kissed or anything. This ex-patient from the Center, a guy who wanted me, was jealous of Peri. He followed her around. One day, I was supposed to meet Peri in a park, but she never showed up. He'd strangled her.

The lie sort of worked, the way it had with the nurses in the beginning of my hospital stay. I got the compassion I wanted, the look of concern, but I didn't get the truth out.

A lot of people don't want to hear about the hospitals. I can understand this. I don't know how to explain that I'm an ex–mental patient who never had a mental illness. There's no use in insisting you're not crazy. All ex–mental patients seem to be lumped together, schizophrenics, manic-depressives, whatever.

When I was in graduate art school in New York, I'd see this guy, Broadway Bob, he'd sing "Give my regards to Broadway" for spare change. I'd sit on the stoop and have a cigarette with him. He'd circle me and talk to the air: "She's nice, isn't she? I like her, too." He didn't scare me. To me he was a hero. I admired his ability to survive.

Eventually, I got a chance to speak to an audience that wanted to hear my story. A woman called and asked would I be willing to go to Beijing? I thought, Beijing? Beijing where? The International Gay and Lesbian Human Rights Commission paid for me to fly to China for the United Nations Fourth World Conference on Women.

I spoke on a stage at the non-governmental meeting part. It was a tribunal about human rights violations against women. I was shaking up there. When you've had your sanity challenged, you always have something to prove. But I did fine. I told about the hospitals, about putting on eye shadow for points, about being locked up for being an inappropriate female. I told them that some people have said I should have gone along with the doctors, acting the feminine part. But this would have been worse. I would have lost myself.

While I spoke I looked down at my notes the whole time. It wasn't until I'd walked off the stage that I realized that people were clapping. Standing up and clapping. The only standing ovation of the session.

Now I draw and paint all the time. It has saved my life. In one of my first art classes, the assignment was to create a life-size self-portrait. I built a wooden box, one foot square. Inside I put sand and dumbbells that equaled my weight—130 pounds. This was my self-portrait. All of this weight crammed into a box. I carried it into class. My professor was ecstatic. He told me to keep creating. I'd found my place.

I have more than 3,000 paintings; I can't stop myself. Art pours out. I make a living from it. Recently I drew a picture of myself standing by the door inside the seclusion room. I'm looking out the small chicken-wire window. I've got my back to the mattress on the floor, my back to the loneliness of that white room. I can't see much, although once I did see the chubby face of Anne, the multiple-personality screamer who said she might have to kill me. Even so, I'm looking out the window. It's my nature; I have to keep looking out. I'm wearing a Michael Reese hospital gown with three ties in the back and a snap at the top. Fred the lech hasn't yet snuck into my room and rubbed his hands over my body while I'm tied in restraints, but he will. His touch through my hospital gown—it's coming. Looking at the picture I realized it marked the end of something. Often I have to think hard to find a title for a drawing but not this time. The name just came to me. I wrote across the bottom: *The last time I wore a dress.*

The hospitals are in the past, but that's not where they live in my mind. Three or four times a week I have night terrors. Even now, after all these years. I'm running, being chased, or hiding. While I sleep, I curl in on myself, every muscle tensed. I hold my breath. I hold it as long as I can. It's like I'm trying to hold it all in, all the feelings about the nurse coming at me with a syringe of Thorazine, me with my hands and feet tied to the bed and Valerie walking away across the lawn. Then my breath pushes out of me, really hard; it comes out in ragged whimpers. My hands start to move, I claw at my face. If my girlfriend is with me, she'll say, "It's okay, honey, it's a dream," and hold me, but I don't wake up until whatever I'm dreaming has played itself out. Sometimes my stomach is churning so hard I run to the bathroom and throw up. I want to get the churning out, I want everyone out, Frank the hit man, Nurse Kay, the patient who screamed, "I want to die," but they won't go. They're in me, still.

When I get back into bed, I rest my head on the pillow. I try to think of nothing. I practice the trick of going numb, the trick that I perfected in the hospitals, the trick that has bound me to the past. I pretend I don't care. I don't care. When this not-caring works, and I fall into a dreamless sleep, I think I'm lucky. I think I'm finding peace, but I'm not.

ACKNOWLEDGMENTS

MANY PEOPLE have helped to shape my life and, by extension, this book. Foremost I would like to thank my mother, Deborah Bacquel, who passed on to me her formidable survival instincts and gave me courage.

Along the way, my third-grade teacher, Kathy Dickerson, has proved what a tremendous difference an individual can make in the life of a young person. The same can be said of Karen Belsey, the intern from the Wilson Center, who continues to remind me that no matter how bad things get, I can always come over and pick raspberries.

My best friend, Rick Pihl, has been with me through everything and as a debt of gratitude, I have refrained from telling the story of how he accidentally hit me over the head with a bottle.

During the process of writing this book, my girlfriend, Chris, provided me immense comfort through the nightmares, for which I am most appreciative. Andrew, my movie buddy, taught me the art of laughter. Marieka, who helped me to find my voice, encouraged me to follow it.

As always, my friends have sustained me, particularly my brother Anne, Amanda King, Diane W., Tom-Girl, Michele, Miguel, Free, Dawn, Tara, Kari and Sean Donkers, Julie Balogh, Nan Nelson (I miss you), Leslie, Gogi, Miles, Inno, Kristi, Gopal, Annette, Lisa Pihl, Diane and Julie, Eileen and Donn Weipert, Becky and the Smiths, Gayle and Lila, Michael Tunney, Jenni Olson, everyone at Art Explosion especially Anthony, Malia, Shannon, John C., Bryan, Mel, Jonathan, Terri and Geoff, and everyone at Theatre Rino, especially Adele and Iris.

I have found family in unexpected places and for this I thank Pam, Jack, Temple, Claire, and Max Byars as well as Paddy Nolan and the crowd at the Dovre Club, especially Brian, Kim, Cisco, Terry, Gary, Catherine, Ringo, Mathieu, Chris and Chris. My cats Alice and Roxanne have instructed me daily in the meaning of unconditional love.

Four groups were the first to take my story seriously: the National Center for Lesbian Rights, the International Gay and Lesbian Human Rights Commission, the Community United Against Violence and the National Organization for Women. Individuals involved with those groups, including Shannon Minter, Kate Kendell, Julie Dorf, Kagendo, Octavia, Rachel, Sydney, Lester Olmstead-Rose, Jean Morrison, James Hormel and Charlotte Bunch, have my heartfelt thanks.

Also, I'm grateful to the Lonnie Martin Jr. Living Trust for the generous donation that made it possible for me to testify at the Global Tribunal on Accountability for Women's Human Rights in Beijing, China.

For their faith in me, I'd like to thank Glynn Durham, Grannie, Linda Joplin, Tom and Pam Copeland, Mary Kane, Lawrence from the Lawrence L. Hultberg Fine Art Gallery, Jane Dickie from Hope College, Phil and Dino from *Frontiers* Magazine, Denise Kiernan from *The Village Voice*, Erin Blackwell, Charles Flowers and Urvashi Vaid.

And for inspiring me with their strength, I thank Camille, James Greene, Leslie Feinberg, David Harrison, Susan Stryker, Kate Bornstein, Riki Anne Wilchins, Shadow Morton, Kiki Whitlock and Jamie Faye Fenton.

Special thanks to my sister and my new brother-in-law. I also want to thank my father, stepmother and all my extended family for their love and support.

My editor Mary South, my agent Bonnie Nadell, Crystal, and Phyllis Burke were instrumental in bringing this project to life, and I thank them. Perhaps most important, I want to thank my cohort Jane Meredith Adams—hello, hello, hello and hello. We did it.

Anyone wishing to contact me can do so via
   email: lastdress@aol.com
   mail: Daphne Scholinski, PO Box 41-1084, SF, CA, 94141

—Daphne

FOR THEIR COMMENTS, suggestions and encouragement, I am truly grateful to Maureen Bogues, Molly Giles, Graham Hewson, Daphne Kempner, Roger King, Bonnie Nadell, Daphne Northrop, Eric Pfeiffer and Jane Rubin. Special thanks are in order for Crystal Brunzell, Phyllis Burke, Michelle Carter, Nona Caspers, Mary South and, of course, Daphne Scholinski.

Anyone wishing to contact me can do so via
   email: jma1@well.com

—JMA

APPENDIX

Diagnostic criteria for Gender Identity Disorder

A. A strong and persistent cross-gender identification (not merely a desire for any perceived cultural advantages of being the other sex).

In children, the disturbance is manifested by four (or more) of the following:

(1) repeatedly stated desire to be, or insistence that he or she is, the other sex

(2) in boys, preference for cross-dressing or simulating female attire; in girls, insistence on wearing only stereotypical masculine clothing

(3) strong and persistent preferences for cross-sex roles in make-believe play or persistent fantasies of being the other sex

(4) intense desire to participate in the stereotypical games and pastimes of the other sex

(5) strong preference for playmates of the other sex.

In adolescents and adults, the disturbance is manifested by symptoms such as a stated desire to be the other sex, frequent passing as the other sex, desire to live or be treated as the other sex, or the conviction that he or she has the typical feelings and reactions of the other sex.

B. Persistent discomfort with his or her sex or sense of inappropriateness in the gender role of that sex.

In children, the disturbance is manifested by any of the following: in boys, assertion his penis or testes are disgusting or will disappear or the assertion that it would be better not to have a penis, or aversion toward rough-and-tumble play and rejection of male stereotypical toys, games and activities; in girls, rejection of urinating in a sitting position, assertion that she has or will grow a penis, or assertion that she does not want to grow breasts or menstruate, or marked aversion toward normative feminine clothing.

In adolescents and adults, the disturbance is manifested by symptoms such as preoccupation with getting rid of primary and secondary sex characteristics (e.g., request for hormones, surgery, or other procedures to physically alter sexual characteristics to simulate the other sex) or belief that he or she was born the wrong sex.

C. The disturbance is not concurrent with a physical intersex condition.

D. The disturbance causes clinically significant distress or impairment in social, occupational, or other important areas of functioning.

Code based on current age:

302.6 Gender Identity Disorder in Children

302.85 Gender Identity Disorder in Adolescents or Adults

Specify if (for sexually mature individuals)

Sexually Attracted to Males

Sexually Attracted to Females

Sexually Attracted to Both
Sexually Attracted to Neither

From: American Psychiatric Association. *Diagnostic and Statistical Manual of Mental Disorders*, Fourth Edition. Washington, D. C.: American Psychiatric Association, 1994.

RESOURCE LIST

This list is intended to help Lesbian, Gay, Bisexual, Transgendered and Questioning youth and their families to find support and services. Many of the groups listed here can direct you to groups in your own area. Please use these organizations and support them with your time and money.

National Youth Advocacy Coalition
1711 Connecticut Ave. NW , Suite 206, Washington, D.C. 20009
202-319-7596 E-mail: nyouthac@aol.com

National coalition of organizations and agencies serving LGBTQ youth, including national directory of support groups and social services for LGBTQ youth.

National Center for Lesbian Rights—Youth Project
870 Market St., Suite 570, San Francisco, CA 94102
415-392-6257; toll-free line for youth only 1-800-528-6257
E-mail: nclrsf@aol.com

National lesbian, feminist, multicultural legal resource center. Services specific to the Youth Project include information and counseling about legal rights, assistance in accessing youth shelters and social services, and referrals to legal resources, patients' rights advocates, and lesbian, gay, bisexual and transgendered youth groups.

The Hetrick-Martin Institute
2 Astor Place, New York, NY 10003
212-674-2400 E-mail: hmi@hmi.org

Provides an array of services for lesbian, gay, bisexual and transgendered youth, including individual and family counseling; referral services; an after-school drop-in center with discussion and support groups and classes; outreach to homeless and runaway youth; internship programs and a speakers' bureau. Also runs the Harvey Milk School, an alternative high school for lesbian, gay, bisexual and transgendered youth.

Parents, Families and Friends of Lesbians and Gays (PFLAG)
1101 14th Street NW, Suite 1030, Washington, D.C. 20005
202-638-4200 E-mail: info@pflag.org

Provides support, education, and advocacy organization for families and friends of lesbian, gay, bisexual and transgendered people.

International Gay and Lesbian Human Rights Commission (IGLHRC)
1360 Mission St., Suite 200, San Francisco, CA 94103
415-255-8680 E-mail: iglhrc@iglhrc.org

Non-governmental human rights organization, working primarily to monitor, document and mobilize responses to human rights abuses against transgendered people, lesbian, gay or bisexual people, people with HIV and AIDS, and those oppressed due to their sexual identities or sexual conduct with consenting adults.

Community United Against Violence (CUAV)
973 Market St., Suite 500, San Francisco, CA 94103
Hotline: 415-333-HELP

Dedicated to preventing and treating violence against and within the transgendered, lesbian, gay and bisexual communities—with an emphasis on addressing hate violence and domestic violence.

FTM International
1360 Mission St., Suite 200, San Francisco, CA 94103
415-553-5987 E-mail: info@ftm-intl.org
International support group for female-to-male transsexuals (non-hormones and non-op included). Provides information and referrals. Newsletter available by subscription.

American Educational Gender Information Service
PO Box 33724, Decatur, GA 30033-0724
770-939-2128; Helpline 770-939-0244
E-mail: aegis@gender.org Web:http://www.ren.org/rafil/aegis.html
Information and referrals for transgendered and transsexual people.

International Conference on Transgender Law and Employment Policy
P.O. Drawer 35477, Houston, TX 77235
713-777-8452 E-mail: ictlep@aol.com
International legal resource center for transgendered people.

Lambda Legal Defense and Education Fund
120 Wall St., Suite 1500, New York, NY 10005
212-809-8585 E-mail: lldefny@aol.com
Works nationally through test-case litigation and public education to defend the civil rights of lesbians, gay men, and people with HIV/AIDS, including work on preventing harassment and discrimination against lesbian and gay students.

American Civil Liberties Union Lesbian & Gay Rights Project
125 Broad Street, New York, NY 10004
212-944-9800 E-mail: lgrpaclu@aol.com
Web: http://www.aclu.org
Litigation, legislation and other legal work on behalf of lesbians, gay men and bisexuals. Special emphasis on protecting civil rights of lesbian and gay students and teachers.

Gay and Lesbian Advocates and Defenders
294 Washington Street, Suite 740, Boston, MA 02108
617-426-1350 Web: http://www.glad.org
Litigates civil rights cases involving lesbians and gay men in Massachusetts and surrounding states.